Developmental Programming for Infants and Young Children

Volume 1

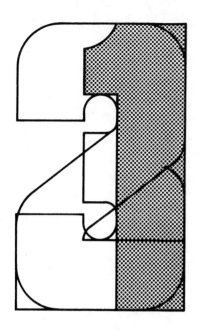

Developmental Programming for Infants and Young Children

D. Sue Schafer and Martha S. Moersch, Editors

Assessment and Application

by Sally J. Rogers and Diane B. D'Eugenio

The University of Michigan Press
Ann Arbor

ISBN 0-472-08771-1
Library of Congress Catalog Card No. 76-49257
Published in the United States of America by
The University of Michigan Press and simultaneously
in Rexdale, Canada, by John Wiley & Sons Canada, Limited
Manufactured in the United States of America

1980   1979   10   9   8   7   6   5   4

Early Intervention Project for Handicapped Infants and Young Children,
Institute for the Study of Mental Retardation and Related Disabilities,
The University of Michigan.

Contents

Assessment

The proliferation of various methods for evaluating treatment/educational effectiveness and the current emphasis on accountability in education have pointed to the need for assessment-based educational programs. Diagnostic and prescriptive teaching, behavioral task analysis, and therapeutic techniques require that each child's level of performance be continuously monitored and that the treatment/educational plans be developed dynamically to meet the child's current and rapidly changing needs. Although there are many assessment instruments and developmental schedules available, there is little information provided with them to help a teacher/therapist bridge the gap between assessment and program planning.

This volume and volume 2, *Early Intervention Developmental Profile,* were designed to reduce the gap between evaluation and programs for children functioning between the 0 to 36-month levels of development. Together these two volumes can help the educator/therapist develop comprehensive and individualized developmental programs by translating comprehensive evaluation data rendered by the profile into short-term behavioral objectives which form the basis of daily activities planned to facilitate emerging skills. Volume 3, *Stimulation Activities*, is a comprehensive collection of sequenced activities from which professionals and parents can select appropriate activities which will blend into the family's daily routine. The final step, that is, the reassessment, completes this continuous, objective process. (Excerpts from volumes 2 and 3 are contained in the Appendix.)

These tools and the educational/treatment process described in this volume were successfully used by therapists, educators, psychologists, and parents for more than fifty handicapped infants and preschoolers between August, 1974, and July, 1976, and effectively promoted developmental accomplishments in a diverse population of very young, handicapped children.

The *Early Intervention Developmental Profile* was conceived in order to fill the need for an instrument that would describe the developmental status of a child in the 0 to 36-month age range in six areas of development. The profile is one of the products of the Early Intervention Project for Handicapped Infants and Young Children, which created an interdisciplinary treatment approach to the developmental problems of exceptional infants. The primary treatment team (occupational therapist, physical therapist, and speech and language pathologist), assisted by a psychologist and a special educator, needed to gather more detailed information about reflexive and cognitive development than was traditionally provided by infant assessment tools. They sought one instrument which contained developmental sequences in cognitive and motor development as well as sensorimotor, language, and social growth, so that the time and repetition involved in administering four or more separate instruments to each infant could be diminished.

In addition, the evaluation instrument needed to fit the assessment-based approach to programming used by the project. The project's approach included frequent (3 month) reevaluations and thus needed a tool which could be administered either by a single trained evaluator or by an interdisciplinary team in a relatively brief period of time (an hour or less) and which would supply detailed information in the six developmental areas while monitoring development of both severely handicapped and more mildly handicapped infants.

Initial compilation of major developmental milestones for ages 0 to 60-months in the six areas mentioned above began in August, 1974, and was first used within the project in December, 1974. The initial profile results led to the formulation of behavioral objectives and helped to strengthen assessment-based programming within the project.

The first profile revision occurred in March, 1975, and included (1) expansion of the gross motor scale to include a far more detailed examination of reflexive development, (2) enlargement of the feeding skills scale of the self-care section to include oral motor development, and (3) minor changes on the other scales. At this point, the profile had stimulated the interest of numerous other professionals engaged in education of handicapped infants and preschoolers. Increasing requests for the profile prompted the project to consider wider distribution and eventual publication of the profile. Thus, the final critical examination of the profile began in late 1975.

The final revision carefully considered the retention of the 36 to 60-month items, which seemed to duplicate several already-existing and satisfactory preschool assessment instruments (e.g., Sanford, 1973; Doll, 1966). Rather than duplicate existing materials, the profile was revised to include only the 0 to 36-month-age range since this part of the profile met a real need in bringing together the various aspects of infant development. In addition, the final revision, which was completed in November, 1975, expanded the social/emotional scale to include aspects of theory from attachment and ego psychology literature, and enlarged the self-care scales to describe the development of feeding, toileting, and dressing/hygiene skills in greater detail. The final profile revision has been in use since December, 1975.

Description and Purpose of the Profile

The *Early Intervention Developmental Profile* is an infant assessment instrument made up of six scales which provide developmental norms and milestones in the following areas: perceptual/fine motor, cognition, language, social/emotional, self-care (feeding, toileting, and dressing/hygiene), and gross motor development. The profile contains 274 items and can be administered in less than an hour by an experienced evaluator or multidisciplinary team. The profile yields needed information for planning comprehensive developmental programs for children with all types of handicaps who function below the 36-month-age level. It is intended to supplement, not replace, standard psychological, motor, and language evaluation data.

Information which describes the child's skills on the testing day is provided by use of the profile; it does not supply data which can predict future capabilities or handicaps. The profile should not be used to diagnose handicapping conditions, such as mental retardation, emotional disturbance, or cerebral palsy. However, by providing a convenient tool which examines a child's skills in six different areas, the profile aids in describing the child's comprehensive functioning and in identifying his relative strengths and weaknesses. It also indicates which developmental skills are expected to emerge next in a normal sequence. Identification of emerging skills allows for a close "match" between the child's readiness and his program so that appropriate activities can be planned to facilitate the emergence of slightly higher skills.

The profile has several unique features. First, the combined results of the six scales provide a comprehensive record of the child's skills, the breadth of which is not found in other infant evaluation tools. Second, the completed profile lends itself well to the formulation of individualized objectives, a necessary ingredient of programming for handicapped infants and young children. Third, the profile not only compiles a variety of developmental milestones, as seen in the language and self-care scales, but also reflects current developmental theory in the motor, cognitive, and social areas. The gross motor scale and the feeding section of the self-care scale reflect a body of knowledge which constitutes the basis for the current treatment of cerebral palsy in infants and young children (e.g., Bobath, 1969; Fiorentino, 1972) by emphasizing neurodevelopmental theories of reflexive development, the integration of primitive reflexes into higher order balance, and equilibrium responses. The cognition scale provides landmarks in the development of sensorimotor intelligence described by Piaget (1954) and validated by a host of studies in infant cognition over the last ten years (e.g., Giblen, 1971; Gratch and Landers, 1971). The cognition scale focuses specifically on the acquisition of the concepts of object permanence, causal relationships, spatial relationships, and imitation during the first two years of life. The social/emotional scale reflects current theory on the emotional attachment between the mother and child and the child's gradual acquisition of ego functions during the first 36 months of life (e.g., Mahler, Pine, and Bergman, 1975).

Formulation and Validation of the Scales

Item selection began with a review of well-known, standardized infant evaluation instruments, including general developmental scales, motor scales, and language scales. The selection criteria for items included the following: first, an item must either have appeared in at least two recognized scales, or must be an original item, appearing in no other scale. This latter stipulation allowed the authors to develop original items based on current developmental theories. Second, each item was scrutinized by the project staff member most highly trained in each area of development (e.g., psychologist for the cognition scale; physical therapist for the gross motor scale, etc.) to determine whether it represented a major developmental milestone rather than an unimportant or incidental skill acquisition. Third, the items selected for each section had to represent all aspects of development for that section. For example, the language scale had to include both receptive and expressive items (both gestural and oral modes). And finally, several items had to represent the developmental accomplishments acquired during each age range appearing in the profile: 0 to 2, 3 to 5, 6 to 8, 9 to 11, 12 to 15, 16 to 19, 20 to 23, 24 to 27, 28 to 31, and 32 to 35 months. These age groupings, which cover a 3-month span in the first year and a 4-month span in the second and third years, were used for each scale except the toileting and dressing/hygiene sections of the self-care scale in which items begin at the 12-month level, and the cognition scale, in which Piaget's suggestion of age grouping was followed through the second year. It is important to note that no consistent attempt was made to arrange items within age ranges in developmental sequence.

Age Norms

The profile has not been standardized on a normal or an exceptional population of infants and young children. Thus, items were not selected for specific age groupings based on results of children's performances in the profile. Rather, assignment of items to specific age ranges was based on standardizations or research from other instruments. The age norms of items which appeared on two or more standardized scales were averaged, and the result determined the age-range placement on the profile. Even though this procedure allowed less thoroughly standardized instruments to carry the same weight as better standardized instruments, it was felt that the age groupings were broad enough to smooth out most differences. For original items, such as the Piagetian-based cognitive items, the age-norm suggestions of the original source, i.e., Piaget (1954), were used. The process by which items were placed in age groupings further bears out the need to use standardized instruments when *diagnosis* of developmental level is required; profile data can provide only a general estimate.

Validation Studies

Concurrent validity of the profile was examined by correlating each of the six profile scales with standardized, widely used evaluation instruments. A developmental level was attained for each of fourteen handicapped children after evaluation on each of the six profile scales,[1] following the scoring procedures described on page 9. These profile results were correlated with the developmental results of formal disciplinary evaluations by psychology, physical or occupational therapy, and speech and language, which had been administered no more than a month preceding or following the date of the profile examination.

As table 1 indicates, the correlation coefficients for all the scales were generally high, ranging from a low of .33 between the profile gross motor scale and Receptive-Expressive Emergent Lan-

---

1. Scores from the three sections of the self-care scale were combined to give one developmental level for that scale.

guage (REEL) scale, and a high of .96 between the profile social scale and the Bayley Mental scale and between the profile cognition scale and the Bayley Mental scale. The profile gross motor scale was handled slightly differently. Because gross motor evaluations traditionally rely on clinical judgment rather than a standardized instrument per se, the profile gross motor scale was correlated with the results of clinical motor evaluations as well as with the Bayley Motor scale, with the resulting correlations .95 and .84, respectively.

TABLE 1

Correlation Coefficients Between Developmental Levels
Attained on the Profile and on Standardized Instruments

Profile Scale	Bayley Mental Scale (N = 13)	Bayley Motor Scale (N = 7)	Vineland Social Maturity Scale (N = 12)	REEL (N = 11)	Clinical Motor Evaluation (N = 14)
Cognition	.96***	.82***	.90***	.55	.68
Perceptual/Fine Motor	.91***	.84***	.93***	.44	.82*
Gross Motor	.87***	.95*	.84***	.33	.84*
Language	.90***	.62*	.85***	.75**	.36
Social/Emotional	.96***a	.88***	.91***b	.51	.83*
Self-care	.80**	.66**	.77**	.55	.81*c

***p $\leq$ .001   a: N = 12
 **p $\leq$ .01   b: N = 11
  *p $\leq$ .05   c: N = 13

Although measurements of different aspects of normal infant development typically show high correlations, a population of handicapped infants may deviate from normal expectancies. The relationships among the profile's six scales were explored to determine the consistency of individual performances across the six scales. The profile results for the fourteen children noted above were scored, and developmental levels were assigned for each of the six scales. The correlation coefficients were relatively high, ranging from a low of .59 among the language, self-care, and gross motor scales to a high of .95 between the cognition and social/emotional scales (see table 2). These high correlations can be interpreted in two ways. First, high correlations among various infant scales appear throughout the developmental literature and may reflect (a) a strong unitary factor in infant development which is relatively undifferentiated when compared to more mature intellectual functioning; and/or (b) the dependence of the performance of cognitive, social, and language tasks on both gross and fine motor functioning in normal infant development. However, one might expect to see lower relationships among the six scales within the handicapped infant population than was found here since those children's functioning on one or more scales might be grossly impaired by a handicapping condition. It may well be that the number of subjects used in this study was too few for such trends to emerge.

Interrater reliability was examined using a tester-observer paradigm. The tester (project psychologist) videotaped three profile assessments. These evaluations provided a total of 100 profile items which were considered clear enough to score. Nine raters trained in profile administration and experienced in evaluation and treatment of young handicapped children served as the observers. Each observer scored the same 100 profile items via videotape replay. Each observer's results were compared to the tester's which served as the scoring criterion. The percent of agreement between tester and observers ranged from a low of 80 percent to a high of 97 percent, with a mean of 89 percent agreement overall.

In order to examine the amount of unexpected change in a child's profile scores over time, the results of profile assessments for fifteen children were examined. Each child was administered the

TABLE 2

Correlation Coefficients Among the Six Profile Scales

	Self-care (N = 14)	Social/ Emotional (N = 13)	Language (N = 14)	Gross Motor (N = 14)	Perceptual/ Fine Motor (N = 14)
Cognition	.73**	.95***	.89***	.81***	.90***
Perceptual/Fine Motor	.87***	.93***	.72**	.87***	
Gross Motor	.74**	.91***	.59*		
Language	.59*	.83***			
Social Emotional	.85***a				

***p ≤ .001
**p ≤ .01   a: N = 13
*p ≤ .05

profile three times, at 3-month intervals. For some children, the same rater administered all three assessments; for others, the rater varied from one examination to another. All raters, however, had established acceptable interrater agreement beforehand. Each child's initial scores on each of the six profile scales were compared to scores on retests given at 3 and 6 months. As seen in table 3, the correlations between the initial scores and each retest score are uniformly high and are significant at both the $p < .01$ and $p < .001$ levels.

TABLE 3

Correlation Coefficients for Profile Test and Retests
at Three- and Six-Month Intervals

Profile Scale	N	Rank Order Correlation (Gamma)	Pearson Product-Moment Correlation (r)
		Test and Three-Month Retest	
Language	15	.83**	.93*
Social/Emotional	15	.96**	.98*
Self-care	13	.92**	.98*
Cognition	14	.95**	.97*
Perceptual/Fine Motor	15	.96**	.98*
Gross Motor	15	.92**	.97*
		Test and Six-Month Retest	
Language	12	.77**	.93*
Social/Emotional	12	.93**	.97*
Self-care	12	.87**	.95*
Cognition	11	.77**	.90*
Perceptual/Fine Motor	12	.91**	.97*
Gross Motor	12	.84**	.96*

**p ≤ .001
*p ≤ .01

Administration, Scoring, and Interpretation

The profile was designed to be administered by a multidisciplinary team which includes a psychologist or special educator, physical or occupational therapist, and a speech and language therapist. These disciplines can provide the expertise which the profile requires for the language, cognitive, reflexive, and oral-motor items. Even within these stated disciplines, some competent practitioners may not be well acquainted with some of the items or age ranges included on the profile, so that careful reading of the profile and this volume as well as experience with actual assessment techniques are recommended.

Training several multidisciplinary teams to administer the profile has helped the project develop a successful instructional procedure which includes (1) thorough familiarization of each team member with all the items in his particular disciplinary scale; followed by (2) a team evaluation of a normal infant or toddler, with each team member administering his disciplinary scale item by item, explaining terminology, administration techniques, and scoring criteria to the other team members; (3) repetition of number 2 several times in order to observe normal handling of test items by the children; and (4) a team evaluation of one or more handicapped infants and young children.

As seen by the high tester-observer reliabilities, the authors have found it is possible for each team member to learn to administer the entire profile, rather than to be limited by one's disciplinary skills to only certain scales. The process of learning to administer the entire profile can result in each team member's growth in respect for the other's skills as well as in his overall competence and knowledge of the breadth and richness of early development. This interdisciplinary training process should begin after each team member has become thoroughly comfortable with his own discipline-related scales. A team member then should pair with a nondisciplinary counterpart for an evaluation of a normal child, at which time each teaches the other his discipline-related scales, supervises administration and scoring, explains techniques, and answers questions. When high proficiency and agreement have been obtained between the two, pairing should be changed and the process repeated for each new pair. The final step is attempting a total evaluation by each team member of one or more children in a situation where all team members could be called upon when needed.

Once all the members of the evaluation team have become familiar with the profile, all six scales can usually be administered in less than an hour. The assessment should take place at a time when the child is usually active and happy, and the schedule should be flexible enough to allow for changing, feeding, and other infant needs. The profile can be administered in the child's home or in a clinical setting. In either case, the evaluation room should be comfortable, quiet, and, if possible, small and free of other stimulating materials so that the child's attention can be held by the evaluation items. A nonambulatory child will require a mat on the floor or on a table as well as a chair and table at which the mother can hold the child on her lap. An ambulatory child generally pays better attention seated at a small table. The evaluation should take place with the child's parent(s) or care giver(s) present. Their role can be as active as is comfortable for them, and they can participate by assisting with item administration as well as by answering some questions from the social/emotional and self-care scales. The evaluator should test each item unless the test-item descriptions described in pages 15-42 indicate that the item can be scored via interview.

The materials needed for profile administration are listed in the Introduction to volume 2, *Early Intervention Developmental Profile*. Almost all the materials can be found commercially. It is strongly recommended that the listed materials be assembled into small suitcases or kits so that the materials can be on hand and readily transportable for home visits, screenings, and other evaluations.

Administration

Administration of the profile typically begins with a brief period of observation of aspects of the child's motor function which may affect the child's performance on the profile. Motor abnormalities should be noted on the profile so that appropriate relaxation and/or positioning techniques can be applied to facilitate the child's optimum performance throughout the evaluation. A workable order for profile assessment begins with the perceptual/fine motor and cognition scales since those items are particularly interesting for young children. Since young children tire easily in a structured situation, it is critical that the child's range of functioning on each of the scales be quickly determined and that the items within that range are adequately covered. This process is facilitated by beginning with an open-ended activity which is scorable at several levels. The use of 1-inch colored cubes is suggested for two reasons. First, they are generally interesting to the child, whose spontaneous handling of the cubes often provides scorable responses. Second, because cube items exist at almost every age level on the profile, the child's highest level of success on cube items will give the tester a guide as to which age ranges should be explored. Using the sequential arrangements of items according to materials listed in table 4, the cube items should be administered in ascending order, from easiest to most difficult. The tester should administer all other perceptual/fine motor items within the age range which contains the child's highest success with the cubes. Various items should be administered using the same toy as long as the child is interested, and materials should be changed in order to maintain the child's attention.

The language scale is best administered later in the evaluation so that there has been time for the child to become comfortable and so that spontaneous vocalizations occurring earlier in the evaluation can be recorded and scored on the language scale as they occur. Items from the social/emotional and self-care scales can be administered whenever a break for either the child or parent is needed during the assessment. Gross motor items are administered last for the following reasons. Some children become quite active during the gross motor evaluation, which is thus a nice change of pace from the more structured items; others become quite upset during the gross motor evaluation, and the rapport needed for the other scales is difficult to reestablish once the child has become upset. Parents generally appreciate brief explanations of the tasks, particularly when the child is not succeeding. A brief general statement about the child's performance in terms of his strengths as well as his weaknesses is generally appreciated.

Ceiling and Basal Levels

Once testing has focused on a particular range of items in one developmental scale, more difficult items in that range should continue to be presented until the child has failed either six consecutive items or all items in two consecutive age ranges. This process establishes the *ceiling level* for that scale, i.e., the age range containing the child's highest passed item. A *basal level*, the age range preceding the child's earliest failure, should then be established for the same scale by administering progressively easier (earlier) items until the child passes all items in two consecutive age ranges or until the child passes six consecutive items. The ceiling and basal levels define a range of items on which the child's performance is inconsistent, i.e., a range where passes, pass/fails, and failures occur. This range will provide the focus for programming efforts which are described in the following section of this volume.

Once the ceiling and basal levels have been established on the perceptual/fine motor scale, administer the cognitive, social/emotional, language, self-care, and gross motor items. The basal age level attained on the perceptual/fine motor scale can suggest the age range in which testing on the other scales may begin.

Scoring

Based on accepted disciplinary practice, standard evaluation and scoring techniques for each profile item are provided. Administer each profile item as described on pages 15-42. Score an item *pass* (P) when the criteria are met; score an item *fail* (F) when the child's behavior on an item clearly does not meet scoring criteria. When there is a question as to whether or not the child's behavior on an item has fully met the scoring criteria, a *pass-fail* (PF) can be used to indicate the emergence of the skill measured by that particular item. A final scoring category, *omitted* (O), is used when the evalu-

TABLE 4

Profile Items Administered with the Same Materials

Materials	0-2	3-5	6-8	9-11	12-15	16-19	20-23	24-27	28-31	31-35
						Age Range (in months)				
Ball		44 (C)* 4 (P)			246 (G)		65 (C)	263 (G)	266 (G)	
Bell, rattle	74 (L) 76 (L) 43 (C)									
Book				56 (C)	21 (P)					
Baby bottle		145 (SC) 146 (SC)	154 (SC) 49 (C)	54 (C) 57 (C)						
Cloth			46 (C) 48 (C)	54 (C)		58 (C)				
Crayon				19 (P) 20 (P)	25 (P)	29 (P)	31 (P) 34 (P)	36 (P)		39 (P)
1-inch cube		6 (P) 8 (P) 9 (P)	11 (P) 13 (P)	17 (P)	24 (P) 59 (C) 60 (C)	27 (P)	33 (P)	37 (P) 68 (C) 70 (C)	38 (P)	
Cup						58 (C) 59 (C)	64 (C)		101 (L)	104 (L)
Doll						90 (L) 92 (L)				
Formboard						28 (P)	32 (P)			
Mirror		119 (S)	124 (S)							
Paper							35 (P)			40 (P)
Pegboard			14 (P) 16 (P)		23 (P)	26 (P)	30 (P)			
Raisin (pellet)			12 (P) 15 (P)	18 (P)		61 (C)				
Ring on string	1 (P)	3 (P)	52 (C)				67 (C)			

*Each entry indicates the item number on the profile. The letter in parenthesis indicates the profile scale to which the item belongs: (C) Cognition; (G) Gross Motor; (L) Language; (P) Perceptual/Fine Motor; (S) Social/Emotional; (SC) Self-care.

ator has to omit an item. Omissions are occasionally necessary due to the nature of the child's handicapping condition. For example, some profile items are based on specific sensory modalities, i.e., visual tracking requires visual abilities; localization of sounds requires auditory ability. On these specific items, an O would be scored for the blind and deaf child, respectively. However, when an item can be presented and passed by substituting another sensory modality, i.e., substituting auditorially directed reaching for visually directed reaching for a blind child; substituting sign and gestures for words for a deaf child, the substitution should be used and noted in the scoring section and an O should not be used. Because an O represents the failure of a child to acquire a certain skill due to the nature of his handicap, an O is counted as a failure when establishing basal and ceiling levels.

Reduction of Results

At times, it may be useful to reduce the span of successes and failures on each of the six scales to a single age level for the child in each developmental area. It is critical to note that the resulting developmental level *in no way indicates a mental age* but represents a condensation of the child's general performance on each profile scale. This process allows a comparison of the child's performances across the six scales, but results in loss of information and detail that is needed for individualized program development. The following method can be used to determine the child's approximate performance level on each of the six profile scales:

1. Note the basal level on each scale (the age range preceding the child's lowest failure).
2. Assign the highest number of months in that age range to the child, i.e., for 6 to 8-month age range, assign 8 months; for 24 to 27-month range, assign 27 months.
3. Add the number of P's and PF's that appear above the basal level, counting each pass equal to one point and each PF equal to one-half point.
4. Count the number of items in the next age range and divide by the number of months in that range (e.g., 0-2 = 3 months; 24-27 = 4 months), resulting in the number of items per month.
5. If the total of step 3 is smaller than or equal to the number of items in the next age range (the first part of step 4), then divide the results of step 3 by the results of step 4.
6. Add the results of step 5 to those of step 2. This number provides a performance level, expressed in months, for each scale.
7. If the total of the child's P's and PF's above the basal (step 3) is larger than the number of items in the next age level, then treat the next age level as if it were the basal level, and repeat steps 2 through 5.

Table 5 illustrates steps 1 through 6 of this process.

Use of Profile Graph

The graph on the inside back cover of volume 2 can be used to chart the child's performances on each of the profile scales. This chart will provide a visual portrayal of the child's strengths, weaknesses, and general developmental pattern at the time of evaluation. The graph can be filled out after each evaluation using a different color or pattern of lines. Each line should be dated to illustrate the child's changes over time.

Two methods can be used to complete the graph. One method consists of marking the highest item number on which the child earned a pass[2] on each of the scales, and connecting the points. Thus, the higher points on the graph represent the child's relative strengths; the lower points represent the relatively weak areas. The horizontal lines within which the points fall represent general developmental levels and are noted in months on the left side of the graph. This method is simple

---

2. The pass (P) should be part of a fairly consistent set of P's. An isolated P preceded by several F's should not be used.

TABLE 5

Methodology for Determining Developmental Level
in the Language Scale of the Profile

Results from Evaluation		
Age Range	Profile Item Number	Score
3-5 months	75	P
	76	P
	77	P
	78	P
6-8 months	79	P
	80	F
9-11 months	81	P
	82	F
	83	F
12-15 months	84	F
	85	F
	86	F
	87	F

Steps in Determining Developmental Level

Step 1.   Basal level = 3-5 months

Step 2.   Highest number of months in basal level = 5

Step 3.   Count of P's (P=1) and PF's (PF=½) above basal level = 2

Step 4. $\dfrac{2 \text{ (number of items in 6-8 month level)}}{3 \text{ (number of months in 6-8 month level)}}$ = .67 items/month

Step 5. $\dfrac{2 \text{ (result of step 3)}}{.67 \text{ (result of step 4)}}$ = 3

Step 6.   3 (result of step 5) + 5 (result of step 2) = 8

Therefore, the general developmental level on this language scale is 8 months.

and requires little time. However, since each point on the graph represents the child's highest success, the graph represents the child's *highest* level of performance without consideration for intermittent failures.

A second method involves determining the child's performance level on each scale by using the method described on page 9. Although the profile graph was not designed specifically for this process, it can be adapted in the following way: For each scale, place a mark in the item columns which represent the relative position of the performance level in relation to each age range. For example, a level of 7 months would be marked in the center of each 6 to 8-month range on the appropriate scale. This method is relatively complex when compared with the first. However, the resulting profile of scores will reflect the child's total performance since both passes and failures are considered.

Table 6 illustrates an example of a completed profile graph which is plotted using the first method described above.

TABLE 6
Plotted Profile Graph

Name __M.H.__   Birth Date __January 9, 1974__

Evaluation Dates __July 17, 1975 ; September 15, 1975 ; December 8, 1975__

Developmental Level in Months	Perceptual/ Fine Motor	Cognition	Language	Social/ Emotional	Self-care			Gross Motor
					Feeding	Toileting	Dressing	
32-35	40* ↑ 39	73	107 ↑ 103	142 ↑ 140	171		190 ↑ 188	274 ↑ 269
28-31	38	72 71	102 101	139	170	178	187	268 ↑ 265
24-27	37 36	70 ↑ 68	100 ↑ 96	138 ↑ 136	169	177 176	186	264 ↑ 261
20-23	35 ↑ 30	67 ↑ 64	95	135 ↑ 132	168	175	185 ↑ 183	260 ↑ 258
16-19	29 ↑ 26	63 ↑	94	131	167 ↑ 165	174	182	257 ↑ 250
12-15	25 ↑ 21	58	87 ↑ 84	130 ↑ 129	164 ↑ 162	173 172	181 ↑ 179	249 ↑ 244
9-11	20 ↑ 16	57 ↑ 52	83 ↑ 81	128 ↑ 125	161 ↑ 155			243 ↑ 235
6-8	15 ↑ 11	51 ↑ 46	80 79	124 ↑ 121	154 ↑ 149			234 ↑ 210
3-5	10 ↑ 2	45 ↑ 42	78 ↑ 75	120 ↑ 112	148 ↑ 143			209 ↑ 199
0-2	1	41	74	111 ↑ 108				198 ↑ 191

*Profile item numbers

:::::::::::: July 17, 1975

– – – – – September 15, 1975

———— December 8, 1975

Test Item Descriptions

Perceptual/Fine Motor

1. *Follows moving object past midline*

   With the child on his back and gazing at a ring on a string approximately 8 inches from his face, move the ring horizontally. Score if the child visually tracks the ring's horizontal movement.

2. *Integration of grasp reflex*

   With the child's head at midline, distally move an object across the child's palm. Score if the fingers remain open, i.e., do not immediately grip the object in response to the stimulus.

3. *Reaches for dangling object*

   Hold the ring 12 inches above the child's chest while he is on his back. Score if the child makes arm movements in the direction of the ring.

4. *Moves head to track moving object*

   Seat the child at a table. Place a large or small ball on the table to the child's right and attract his visual attention to the ball. Roll the ball slowly across the table while he watches, repeating three times. Score if the child turns his head to visually track the ball.

5. *Fingers own hands in play at midline*

   Observe the child without toys in his hand. Score if, at any point, the child is seen to explore one hand or finger with his other hand.

6. *Uses ulnar palmar prehension*

   Place a 1-inch cube on the table and attract the child's interest so that he grasps the cube. (If he does not grasp it, place it in either hand.) Score if the child holds the cube with a grasp in which the ulnar three fingers predominate, and the thumb remains adducted and inactive.

7. *Looks at hands*

   Score if at any point the child is seen to watch his hands attentively.

8. *Reaches for cube and touches it*

   Place a 1-inch cube within the child's reach and attract his attention to it. Score if the child makes approach movements with his arms which result in his making contact with the cube.

9. *Uses radial palmar prehension (uses thumb and two fingers)*

   Administer as in number 6. Score if the child holds the cube in his palm with his radial fingers and thumb even though the thumb is not in complete opposition.

10. *Transfers toy from hand to hand*

    Score if the child is seen to transfer an object from hand to hand two or more times.

11. *Retains two cubes after third is offered*

    Place three 1-inch cubes on a table in front of the child. Encourage the child to pick up one in each hand and then offer him the third cube. Score if the child retains one cube in each hand when the third is offered, or if the child manages to secure all three cubes rather than releasing one to attain the third.

12. *Rakes or scoops up raisin and attains it*

    Place a raisin or a sugar pellet within the child's reach and attract his attention to it. Score if the child manages to attain the raisin using a raking or a scooping movement of the fingers into the palm.

13. *Has complete thumb opposition on cube*

    Administer as in number 6. Score if the child holds the cube between his thumb and fingers with complete opposition of the thumb and without the cube touching the palm.

14. *Pulls one peg out of pegboard*

    Offer the child a pegboard with one or more pegs inserted. If he does not pull any out, demonstrate. Score if he is able to pull one peg out independently.

15. *Uses inferior pincer grasp with raisin*

    Administer as in number 12. Score if the child picks up the raisin or sugar pellet by enveloping the raisin with his thumb against the side of his hand.

16. *Pokes with isolated index finger*

    Place an empty pegboard in front of the child and point out the holes with your index finger. Score if the child places his index finger in one of the holes.

17. *Drops blocks imitatively with no pause before release*

    Demonstrate dropping blocks in a cup one by one. Encourage the child to imitate your actions. Score if he is able to release the blocks into the cup without a pause between positioning his hand and releasing the block.

18. *Uses neat pincer grasp with raisin*

    Administer as in number 12. Score only if the child secures the raisin or sugar pellet with thumb and forefinger opposition.

19. *Attempts to scribble (holds crayon to paper)*

    Place a piece of paper on the table in front of the child. Place a crayon on the paper with the point facing away from the child. Demonstrate drawing with the crayon. Offer the crayon to the child and encourage him to imitate you. Score if the child *touches* the crayon point to the paper, whether or not he leaves a mark.

20. *Holds crayon adaptively (crayon projects out of radial aspect of the hand, one end up and one end down)*

    Administer as in number 19. Score if the child attempts to hold the crayon in writing position with one end to the paper, marking the paper. (Score even if the fist is facing down.)

21. *Turns page of cardboard book*

    Present the child with a cardboard book and encourage him to turn the pages. Score if he manages to turn a page.

22. *Removes cover from small square box*

    Place a toy in the box and show the child how to remove the cover to get the toy. Replace the toy in the box, replace the cover, and encourage the child to remove the cover. Score if the child manages to remove the cover at least twice.

23. *Places one or two pegs in pegboard*

Present a pegboard to the child with all the pegs in place. Remove the pegs, placing them in front of the child. Encourage the child to place the pegs in the holes. Score if the child places one peg two or more times in any hole.

24. *Builds two-cube tower*

Place some cubes in front of the child, and demonstrate tower building. Encourage the child to do the same. Score if the child manages to place one cube on top of another.

25. *Scribbles spontaneously (no demonstration)*

Administer as in number 19, but before demonstrating use of the crayon, allow the child to initiate activity. Score if the child marks on paper *without* a demonstration or instruction.

26. *Places six pegs in pegboard without help*

Administer as in number 23. Score if the child places all six pegs in the holes without help.

27. *Builds three-cube tower*

Administer as in number 24. Score if the child stacks three cubes without a demonstration.

28. *Places round form in formboard (three forms presented)*

Place a completed formboard in front of the child with the round form closest to him. Remove all the forms and place them beneath the formboard directly in front of their respective holes. Encourage the child to put them back in their places. Score if the child places the round form in the correct hole.

29. *Imitates crayon stroke (crayon gripped with butt end firmly in palm)*

Administer after item number 25. Take a crayon from the child and demonstrate drawing a straight, vertical line moving the crayon away from the child. Demonstrate twice. Then ask the child to make a line like yours. Score if the child makes a definite stroke in any direction.

30. *Places six pegs in pegboard in 34 seconds*

Administer as in number 23. Time the child's efforts in three trials, and score if any trial was completed in 34 seconds or less.

31. *Makes vertical and circular scribble after demonstration*

After administering item number 29, take a crayon and demonstrate making circular strokes. Score if the child can imitate both circular scribbles and a stroke.

32. *Completes three-piece formboard*

Administer as in number 28. Score if the child places all three forms in their respective holes.

33. *Builds six-cube tower*

Administer as in number 24. Score if he stacks six cubes.

34. *Begins to manipulate crayon with fingers*

    Observe the child as he draws with a crayon. Score if he holds and manipulates the crayon with his fingers rather than in his palm.

35. *Folds paper imitatively*

    Place a piece of paper in front of the child and demonstrate folding it in half. Encourage the child to imitate your actions. Score if the child turns the edge of the paper in an attempt to fold it, whether or not he leaves a crease.

36. *Draws vertical and horizontal strokes imitatively*

    Administer after number 31. Have the child imitate a vertical stroke as described in number 29. After the child has imitated a vertical stroke, immediately demonstrate a horizontal stroke. Score if the child imitates both strokes.

37. *Aligns two or more cubes for train, no smokestack*

    Place three cubes, lined up together and touching, in front of the child. Place a fourth cube on top of one of the end cubes, telling the child that you are building a train. When the fourth cube is placed, slowly push the train around, making appropriate train sounds. Give the child four more cubes, encouraging him to build a train like yours. Score if the child manages to align at least two cubes in imitation of the train.

38. *Builds eight-cube tower*

    Administer as before. Score if child manages to balance eight cubes in a tower.

39. *Copies a circle already drawn*

    Unseen by the child, draw a circle on a piece of paper with a crayon. Then present a clean piece of paper, a crayon, and the drawn circle to the child. Ask him to draw a circle just like the one on the paper. Score if he draws a closed circle with a single line, no sharp angles, and no extreme overlap.

40. *Cuts with scissors*

    Demonstrate use of scissors to the child by cutting fringe and a line on a piece of paper. Then present him with a fresh piece of paper and the scissors. Score if he manages to make a cut with the scissors by inserting the paper between the blades and moving the blades with his fingers. Score even if his attempt is quite uncoordinated.

41. *Uses adaptive movements rather than reflexive reactions*

Any examples of learned reactions can be scored. Such learned responses would include smiling in response to social stimuli, anticipatory feeding movements while child is being positioned at the breast or bottle, rudimentary hand-to-mouth patterns, or other learned behavior that occurs in response to an external stimulus.

42. *Demonstrates vocal contagion*

Imitate the child's vocalizations immediately after he makes them. Score if the child continues to vocalize after your imitations.

43. *Repeats random movements (primary circular reactions)*

Place a rattle or bell in the child's hand while he is fairly active, so that his random movements make the rattle sound. Observe the child's activity after the rattle has sounded, and score if the child's random activities increase, resulting in the rattle being sounded several more times.

44. *Watches place where moving object disappeared*

Catch the child's visual attention with a toy car or ball by rolling it slowly on the table or floor. While the child watches, roll it slowly behind an open book or other screen. Score if the child watches the point where the toy disappeared behind the book for it to return.

45. *Coordinates two actions in play*

Observe the child in play and score if the child combines two activities simultaneously, such as reach and grasp, grasp and mouth, turning toward a sound, watching while moving hand.

46. *Attains partially hidden object*

Focus the child's attention on a toy. While the child is watching, cover the toy with a cloth so that the child can see only a portion of the toy. Score if the child removes the cloth and attains the toy. (For children unable to lift the cloth, a response may be scored for eye pointing by the child.)

47. *Looks to the floor when something falls*

Hold a sponge in the air and attract the child's visual attention to it. Drop the sponge and note whether the child tracks the sponge as it falls or whether he looks to the floor before the sponge lands. Score if the child shows he knows that the sponge will land on the floor by looking to the floor and waiting for the sponge to land there.

48. *Uncovers face*

Place a cloth over the child's face in a game of peek-a-boo. Score if the child pulls the cloth off his head.

49. *Rotates a bottle inverted less than 180° to drink*

Hold the child's bottle upright at a 90° angle from him with the nipple visible to him and offer him the bottle. Score if the child takes the bottle and inverts it to the proper angle for drinking with nipple toward mouth.

50. *Acts to have pleasurable interaction repeated*

Hold the child on your lap and bounce him, tickle him, etc. When the child is clearly enjoying the activity, stop and pause for about ten seconds. Repeat the sequence and pause again. Repeat a third time and pause, this time wait to see if the child moves in some way to show that he wants the action resumed. Score if he acts in some way, such as by leaning toward you, bouncing his body, moving his arms, to cue you to resume the activity.

51. *Imitates sounds or hand movements already in his repertoire*

Observe the child's play to see what hand movements (such as clapping or banging) and sounds he has in his repertoire. When you have his attention, perform a movement or sound from his repertoire. Score if the child imitates your model.

52. *Pulls string to secure ring and succeeds*

Dangle a ring on a string in front of the child. Then place the ring on the table with the ring beyond the child's reach and the string near his head. Score if the child pulls the string and grasps the ring as it comes within his reach.

53. *Imitates facial movements inexactly*

Make a simple facial movement while the child is watching you, such as sticking out your tongue, patting your mouth, pursing lips. Score if the child clearly attempts to imitate you, though the imitation may be inexact.

54. *Attains completely hidden object (single visible displacements)*

Focus the child's attention on a toy. While the child is watching, cover the toy completely with a cloth and ask the child to retrieve the toy. Score if the child lifts the cloth and attains the toy. (For children unable to lift the cloth, a response may be scored for eye pointing by the child.)

55. *Imperfectly imitates sounds or movements never performed before*

Make a sound or hand movement which the child has not performed before, such as wiggling fingers, rotating wrists, bumping elbows on table, Bronx cheer sound. Score if the child imitates the sound or movement even if the imitation is inexact.

56. *Shows knowledge of toy hidden behind a screen*

Focus the child's attention on an object. Place a book or screen in front of the object while the child is watching. Score if the child reaches over or around the book or removes the book and attains the object.

57. *Rotates a bottle inverted 180° to drink*

Hold the child's bottle with the nipple facing away from the child so that he cannot see it. Hand the child the bottle in this position; score if the child rotates the bottle into feeding position and places the nipple in his mouth.

58. *Repeatedly finds toy when hidden under one of several covers (multiple visible displacements)*

Focus the child's attention on a toy in front of him. While the child watches, place the toy under one of two or three cloths or cups lined up in front of him. If the child immediately retrieves the toy under the proper cup, hide it again under another cup. Score if the child finds the toy immediately in two or more hiding places.

59. *Balances eight 1-inch cubes in a coffee cup*

Place nine 1-inch cubes and a cup in front of the child. Put one cube in the cup, and urge the child to place the remaining cubes in the cup. Score if the child balances all the cubes in the cup. (Cubes will be above cup's rim when all cubes are in the cup.)

60. *Lifts a 1/2-inch cube off a 1-inch cube cleanly, with pincer grasp*

Place a 1/2-inch cube on a 1-inch cube and attract the child's attention to the smaller cube. Encourage the child to take the smaller cube, and score if he lifts the 1/2-inch cube without touching the larger cube. (Motorically handicapped children may not be able to use a pincer grasp, in which case any action they use that results in moving the small cube without touching the larger one may be scored if it occurs twice.)

61. *Inverts a small vial in order to retrieve raisin*

Place a raisin or sugar pellet in a small clear vial and ask the child to get it out. Score if the child attains the raisin by inverting the vial allowing the raisin to fall out.

62. *Uses a stick to try to attain an object out of reach*

Place a toy slightly out of reach of the child and demonstrate how to use the stick as a tool by pushing the toy with the stick toward the child. Again place the toy out of reach and, giving the child the stick, encourage him to retrieve the toy. Score if the child attempts to move the toy with the stick rather than reaching with his hand or simply banging the toy with the stick.

63. *Uses trial-and-error approach to precisely imitate new sounds, words, or movements*

Administer as in item number 55. Score if the child's imitation begins inaccurately but, after several tries by the child, is accurate.

64. *Deduces location of object from indirect visual cues (invisible displacements)*

Focus the child's attention on a small toy, and then invert a cup over the toy. Slide the cup under one of several cloths placed in front of the child and, leaving the toy under the cloth, slide the cup back to the child, showing him that the cup is now empty. Then ask him where the toy is. If the child finds the toy immediately, repeat the entire sequence, leaving the toy under a different cloth. Score if the child immediately finds the toy in at least two trials. (For children unable to lift the cloth, a response may be scored for eye pointing by the child.)

65. *Anticipates trajectory by detouring around object*

Roll a ball under a bed, sofa, etc., and ask the child to retrieve it. Score if the child detours around the piece of furniture while the ball is still moving and retrieves the ball. Do not score if the child tries to follow the path of the ball under the furniture, or watches until it stops and then detours around the furniture.

66. *Imitates sounds, words, or body movements immediately and exactly without practicing*

Administer as in items number 55 and number 63. Score if the child produces immediate, exact imitations.

67. *Indicates knowledge of cause-effect relationships*

While the child is engaged in an activity, place a ring on a string on the table with the string hanging over the edge of the table near the examiner in such a way that the child can see the ring move without seeing that the examiner's hand is pulling the string. Score if, after the child sees the ring move, he tries to determine what is causing the ring to move, by such means as looking under or around the table, observing the examiner's behavior, etc.

68. *Matches colored blocks (red, yellow, blue, green, black)*

Place the five colored cubes in front of the child in a row, about 1 inch apart, with the black cube on one end. Present the second black cube to the child, and as he watches, slowly move the cube to a position directly beneath and in contact with the first black cube. Then teach the child to match colors by giving him another block and guiding him to the correct match, always having the child place the blocks directly beneath and touching the block of the same color. Continue to guide and correct the child as he learns the task. Score if at any point after the examiner has begun the task by matching the black blocks, the child without any help matches the other four presented to him one at a time and not in order.

69. *Pretends to be engaged in familiar activities (being asleep, telephoning)*

Observe the child's play with toys, such as a telephone or doll. Score if the child engages in "pretending" with the toys such as dialing the phone, hearing it ring, and carrying on a conversation, or pouring and drinking imaginary juice from a pitcher and cup. If this is not observed, ask the child to walk like a doggie, or to pretend to be asleep. Score if the child can pretend to be engaged in such activities.

70. *Understands concept of one*

Give the child several cubes. While holding out your hand to him, ask him to give you one cube. Hold your hand there long enough to determine whether he will stop after he has handed you one. Score if he hands just one cube.

71. *Repeats two digits*

First tell the child to say *dog*. After he does, have him say *six*. If he does, ask him to say *eight, four*. If he does not repeat it exactly, ask him to say *three, five*. Score if he can repeat two digits correctly.

72. *Matches four shapes (circle, square, star, cross)*

Place cards of each of the four shapes in a line an inch or so apart in front of the child. Place the second circle in front of the child and, while he watches, move it directly under the first circle. Place each of the other shapes, one at a time, in front of him, for him to match. If he errs, correct him and repeat the task. Score if at any time the child matches each of the four shapes correctly without intervening errors.

73. *Identifies objects by their use (car, penny, bottle)*

Put a toy car, a penny, and a small baby bottle in a row in front of the child. Ask him, *What do we ride in? What do we buy toys with? What do we use when we're thirsty?* Score if he points to or otherwise indicates the correct toy in response to each question.

74. *Moves limbs, head, eyes in response to voice, noise*

Score if child responds to an auditory stimulus such as a bell, rattle, or voice with a definite change in behavior, such as increasing or decreasing his activity, crying, or blinking.

75. *Vocalizes when talked to or sung to*

Score if the child vocalizes in response to a friendly voice addressing him.

76. *Turns head in direction of voices and sounds*

While the child's attention is focused elsewhere, sound a noisemaker approximately 8 inches from the child's ear and behind peripheral vision range. Score if the child turns his head to the sound on both sides. (*Note*: failure on this task may indicate a hearing loss and is an indication for auditory screening.)

77. *Vocalizes emotions, intonation patterns*

Score if the child varies his vocalizations to indicate satisfaction, distress, hunger, etc.

78. *Exhibits differentiated crying*

Score if the child's cry varies according to his needs—whether he is, for example, hungry, tired, or wet. This can also be scored if the mother indicates that his cries differ.

79. *Imitates speech sounds*

When the child is attending, vocalize a speech sound that you have heard the child produce on his own. Score if the child imitates the sound.

80. *Forms bisyllabic repetitions (ma-ma, ba-ba)*

Score if the child is heard to use any two-syllable repetition of a consonant-vowel combination.

81. *Waves or claps when only verbal cue is given*

If the mother indicates that the child knows any games such as pat-a-cake or bye-bye, use the words that the child knows to encourage him to play the game. Score if, on a verbal cue only, the child waves bye-bye, pats his hands for pat-a-cake, etc.

82. *Imitates nonspeech sounds (click, cough)*

Administer as in item number 79, using a nonspeech sound. Score if the child imitates the sound.

83. *Inhibits activity in response to* no

While child is engaged in an activity that is somewhat inappropriate (such as chewing a crayon, pulling hair, etc.) say *no, no* sternly to the child. Score if the child ceases his activity even momentarily.

84. *Uses appropriate intonation patterns in jargon speech*

Score if the child is heard to use conversational inflections in his jabbering.

85. *Imitates words inexactly*

Score if the child is heard to imitate any words during the evaluation. (Animal noises, such as meow and bow-wow, can also be scored.)

86. *Uses two words meaningfully*

   Score if child is heard to use two recognizable (although perhaps distorted) words meaningfully as in labeling an object or responding to a question.

87. *Uses gestures and other movements to communicate*

   Score if child is observed to communicate his wants through hand or body gestures such as shaking his head to mean *no*, pointing, or pushing something away.

88. *Shows body parts, clothing items, or toys on verbal request*

   Ask the child to show you a toy he is holding. Or, ask him where are his shoes, nose, shirt, etc. Score if the child points to, looks at, or otherwise acknowledges the object that you labeled.

89. *Labels one object*

   Hold a common object, such as a ball, cup, or toy car, in front of the child. Ask him, *What is this?* Score if he is able to name one object.

90. *Follows two simple directions*

   Ask the child to perform a few simple activities with a doll, such as kissing the doll, giving it a drink, putting it to bed, etc. Score if the child carries out two of the requests.

91. *Uses single words to express wants*

   Score if the child is heard to use more than two recognizable words to express his wants rather than for only labeling objects. Examples include up, down, drink.

92. *Points to several body parts (on self or doll)*

   Using a doll, say to the child, *Show me the baby's nose, eyes, mouth.* If the child is not able to point them out ask him where are his own eyes, nose, etc. Score if the child points correctly to at least three body parts.

93. *Names one black and white picture*

   Present a large picture card to the child, pointing to each picture and asking him, *What's that?* Score if the child can name any of the pictures.

94. *Selects two of three common objects*

   Place a box, cup, and saucer in front of the child and ask him to hand each one to you upon request. Score if the child chooses at least two correctly when they are named. Child may respond by eye pointing, hand movements, or grasping.

95. *Begins using simple two-word sentences*

   Score if the child is heard to combine two different words, each denoting a separate concept, to indicate a single idea. Combinations such as *daddy gone, baby cry, want cookie* are acceptable; combinations such as *all gone, bye-bye* are not.

96. *Uses first name when referring to self*

   Show the child his own image in a mirror or point to him and ask him, *Who is that?* or *What's your name?* Score if the child uses his first name in response to the question.

97. *Uses three-word sentences*

Score if the child is heard to produce three-word combinations joined in a sentence that demonstrates use of subject, verb, and object such as, *Me want cookie* or *Baby hurt hand.*

98. *Uses negation,* no

If the child is not heard to use *no* spontaneously, try to elicit the response by asking him a question such as: (showing him a doll) *Is this a book?*; (showing him an empty cup) *Is there any milk in the cup?* Score if the child uses *no* in response.

99. *Uses simple pronouns (I, me, you, mine)*

Score if the child is heard to use any pronouns rather than nouns to describe people or objects, even if use is grammatically incorrect, such as, *Me go.*

100. *Labels at least three common objects or pictures*

Administer as in items number 89 and number 93 using more objects from the kit or picture cards. Score if the child names correctly three or more objects or pictures.

101. *Demonstrates an understanding of two prepositions*

Place two cups in front of the child with one inverted. Ask the child to place an object *in* the cup, *on* the cup, *under* the cup, etc. Score if the child follows at least two of the directions correctly.

102. *Understands body part functions*

Ask the child, *What do you hear with? What do you see with?* Score if he can answer one or more correctly.

103. *Says first and last names*

Ask the child his name, and score if he can state both names. (Prompting for his surname is sometimes necessary.)

104. *Demonstrates an understanding of three prepositions*

Administer as in item number 101. Score if the child follows at least three directions correctly.

105. *Forms questions spontaneously using a verb*

Score if the child is heard to form a question of at least two words, one of which is a verb. Examples of minimal responses are: *Where go?* or *Go home?* or *See baby?*

106. *Follows two-step commands*

Present the child with an instruction containing two unrelated directions, such as *Go open the door and then bring me a block.* Make sure the child listens and the items mentioned are readily available. You may repeat the instruction once before he begins to move, but no more cues can be given after he has started to perform. Score if the instructions are carried out correctly.

107. *Forms or uses plurals*

If the child is not heard to use plurals in his spontaneous language, try to elicit responses by showing him pictures of identical objects in a group. Ask him, *What is in the picture?* Score if he uses any plural nouns correctly. (Deers would be a correct response.)

Social/Emotional

108. *Quiets when picked up*

    Score if the child's crying or fussing ceases or diminishes considerably after someone has picked him up to comfort him.

109. *Quiets to face and voice*

    Score if the child's crying or fussing lessens when a friendly face moves close to him or a friendly voice speaks to him.

110. *Maintains brief periods of eye contact during feeding*

    Score if the child is seen to maintain eye contact briefly with his mother during feeding.

111. *Smiles or vocalizes to talk and touch*

    Lean quite near the child, talking gently and stroking him. Score if the child smiles or vocalizes in response.

112. *Reflects adult's smile without adult verbalizing*

    Before speaking to the child, lean near him with good eye contact and a broad smile. Score if the child smiles in response without receiving auditory or tactile cues from the adult.

113. *Laughs*

    Ask the mother if the child ever laughs out loud. If her response is positive, ask her to elicit his laughter. If she is not sure, ask her to play with her baby in a way he particularly enjoys. Score if the child is heard to laugh or giggle. Pleasurable vocalizations or cooing are not enough to pass this item.

114. *Cries when left alone or put down*

    After the child has been engaged in a pleasant activity while being held by the evaluator or the mother, have the adult put the child down and move away from the child. Score if the child clearly shows his unhappiness at being left by crying and fussing.

115. *Shows awareness of strange environments*

    Observe the child's reactions as he first enters the evaluation setting. Score if the child reacts to the strange setting by quieting, fussing, clinging, or visually examining the setting carefully.

116. *Reaches to familiar people (discriminates strangers)*

    With both the mother and a person who is a stranger to the child present, have each person approach the child with outstretched arms, as if offering to pick up the child. Score if the child clearly discriminates the familiar face from the strange one by extending his arms only to the familiar one, by smiling at mother and frowning or crying at the stranger's approach, by turning away or physically withdrawing from the stranger, etc.

117. *Likes physical play*

    Play with the child by gently holding him up in the air, bouncing him, swinging him. Score if the child communicates his enjoyment by laughing, vocalizing, etc.

118. *Smiles spontaneously*

    Score if the child is observed to smile at an adult before the adult responds *in any way* to the child. The child's smile is thus seen as an invitation to interact.

119. *Smiles at image in mirror*

    Show the child his own face in a mirror. Score if he smiles at the image.

120. *Watches adult walk across room*

    Observe the child's behavior when he sees an adult enter, leave, or move across the room. The mother's movement will elicit this response more strongly than a stranger's. Score if the child visually follows the adult's movement.

121. *Laughs at pat-a-cake and peek-a-boo games*

    Perform such games for the child, or move him through the movements as you recite the words. Score if the child laughs at the activities.

122. *Withdraws or cries when stranger approaches*

    Observe the child's reactions when an unfamiliar person approaches him physically, holding out his arms to the child. Score if the child physically moves away, withdraws, cries, or gives other clear signs of his distress.

123. *Shows dislike when familiar toy is removed*

    When the child is happily engaged in play with a toy, take the toy away. Score if the child actively resists giving up the toy, cries, or otherwise clearly signifies his anger or displeasure.

124. *Pats and touches mirror image*

    Administer as in item number 119. Score if the child touches the mirror surface.

125. *Shows discomfort when separated from mother in strange environment*

    During the evaluation, ask the mother to say goodbye to the child and leave the room while the child watches. Score if the child reacts by crying, trying to follow, or refusing to interact with other adults. His unhappiness should be clearly evident in his reaction to her departure.

126. *Participates in pat-a-cake and peek-a-boo games*

    Demonstrate such games to the child in a playful way. Score if the child actively participates by imitating the hand movements, removing the peek-a-boo screen, etc.

127. *Repeats vocalizations or activity when laughed at*

    When the child begins some game, have the adults in the room laugh, smile, and indicate their enjoyment of his activity. Score if, after the adults react, the child repeats his activity for their approval.

128. *Offers toy but does not release*

    When the child is engaged with some toy, ask him to give it to you and hold out your hand to receive it. Score if the child extends the toy toward your hand, whether or not he actually gives it up.

129. *Offers and releases toy to adult*

    Administer as in item number 128. Score if the child actually releases the toy to the adult, even if he wants it back immediately.

130. *Initiates ball play or social games*

Score if the child is observed trying to draw an adult into an activity by throwing a toy to him or by initiating a social game such as peek-a-boo or pat-a-cake.

131. *Uses mother as secure base, checking back with her frequently*

Observe the child as he initially explores the new setting. Score if, during his explorations in the new setting, he is seen to physically separate from his mother and, during these self-initiated separations, is seen to either visually glance at her face fairly often or physically return to her for brief periods of contact.

132. *Occasionally plays near other children*

Observe the child for 30 minutes in a setting where other children are playing. Score if the child tends to physically position himself near the children for periods, rather than staying near his mother or other adults.

133. *Often clings to or pushes away adult*

Try to determine, either by interviewing the mother or observing the mother-child interactions, whether the child frequently exhibits short periods of difficult behavior in which he is either extremely demanding of mother's time and attention in a whining, clinging, infantile fashion, or is extremely insistent around issues of independence or autonomy, demanding that he do things himself, refusing to be even slightly cooperative. Both types of behavior can be seen in the same child, demonstrating his ambivalence around his growing autonomy. Score if these behavioral patterns are occurring.

134. *Cries when preferred activity is blocked*

This item also concerns the child's growing independence. Where at an earlier age the child could be fairly easily redirected in his activities, at this point the child strongly resists any adult interference in his activities, and rather than be distracted by other preferred activities, he displays his anger when his activities are interfered with by crying, temper tantrums, etc. To test this item, observe the child's reactions when the mother refuses to cooperate with him, as in refusing to pick him up or giving him another cookie. Or, if the mother is willing, ask her to interrupt his play by removing his toy. Score if the described behavior is observed, or if the mother reports that it occurs rather commonly under the above conditions.

135. *Picks up and puts away toys on request*

During the evaluation, ask the child to help you replace some toys in the kit or box from which they came. If testing this item is difficult, ask the mother if the child will put toys away at home upon request. Score if the child cooperates with such requests.

136. *Independently chooses toy and begins to play*

Observe the child in an unstructured play period, perhaps near the end of the evaluation. Score if the child, without any adult direction or attention, seeks out play materials and engages himself in play activities without any need for adult direction or request for adult intervention. If the behavior is not observed, ask the mother if the child selects toys and keeps himself busy at home without direction or intervention for 15 to 30 minutes at a time.

137. *Prefers to play near, but not with, other children*

This item is an extension of number 132. To score this item, the child must show a marked preference for and attraction to other children, though he does not yet play with them interactively. Score if the child keeps physically near other children, perhaps engaging in similar activities, rather than simply observing them from afar or preferring adult company.

138. *Mimics domestic activities*

Observe the child's play with toys that represent household items, such as toy kitchens, brooms, or tools. Score if the child enacts, through his play, adult household chores, such as sweeping, cooking, cleaning, and carpentry.

139. *Stares at or points to sexual differences*

Score if the child indicates he is clearly aware of sexual differences between males and females by pointing to, staring at, or mentioning anatomical differences he observes on children of the opposite sex during toileting, bathing, diapering, or undressing.

140. *Separates from mother easily in strange environment*

This item is most easily tested at the very beginning of the evaluation. When he and his mother first arrive, introduce yourself to the child, tell him that you and he will be playing, show him the playroom (with toys in full view), and show him a seat just outside the door where his mother is to sit. Then ask the mother to be seated and gently invite the child in to play with you, extending a friendly hand. Score if the child is willing to come with you, even if he is rather shy and needs a small amount of encouragement. Do not score if he is so uncomfortable once inside the room that he must seek his mother.

141. *Identifies own sex*

Score item if child indicates own sex by answering yes or no to the question, *Are you a boy?* or if he correctly answers the question, *Are you a girl or a boy?* or if he points to pictures of members of his own sex.

142. *Begins to understand taking turns*

Engage in a game with the child in which sharing is required. Good examples are bean bag toss, sharing a manipulative toy, crayons, and clay. Let the child begin, telling him the two of you will share the toy. After he has played a brief while, tell him it's your turn and gently take the toy from him. Take a short turn, then give it back. Cue the child in this way two or three times. Score if the child willingly gives up the toy after the routine has been established, hands it over when requested, and waits for you to finish before he takes it back.

Self-care

Feeding Skills

143. *Sucks and swallows pureed foods from spoon*

    Score if the child is able to take baby food from a spoon.

144. *Integration of rooting reflex*

    Stroke the corner of the child's mouth lightly toward his cheek. Score if the child neither gives an indication of turning his head in the direction of the stroke nor protrudes his tongue.

145. *Coordinates sucking, swallowing, and breathing*

    Observe the child being bottle-fed or breast-fed, be particularly aware of the nursing pattern. Observe whether the child has to cease sucking in order to swallow, and whether his breathing is irregular during sucking, necessitating the feeder to pause and remove the nipple occasionally to let the child "catch his breath." Score if none of the above is observed, i.e., the child is breathing and sucking smoothly and regularly, and is swallowing frequently without having to stop sucking.

146. *Anticipates feeding with increased activity*

    Observe the child just prior to feeding when he is hungry and the mother approaches him with his food or bottle. Score if the child increases his activity upon seeing his dish or bottle.

147. *Gums or mouths pureed food*

    This item is an extension of number 143. To score this item, observe the child being spoon-fed. Score if the sucking movements of the tongue that were present in item number 143 have been replaced by "chewing" movements involving movement of the jaws, with the tongue moving food back into the mouth rather than protruding in a sucking pattern.

148. *Integration of bite reflex*

    Touch a swizzle stick or a spoon to the child's tongue or front of his gums. Score if the child gives no indication of biting down in response to the touch.

149. *Gums and swallows textured food*

    Give the child a graham cracker or similar food. Score if the child gums the cracker with "chewing" motions and swallows it.

150. *Closes lips on spoon to remove food*

    Observe the child while being spoon-fed. Score if while being fed, the child closes his lips on the spoon to get the food off rather than the feeder removing the food by drawing the spoon across the child's gumline.

151. *Drinks from cup with help*

    Hold a cup containing juice or water to the child's mouth. Score if he is able to close his lips on the cup and swallow liquid without choking or letting it all dribble out of his mouth.

152. *Begins to pick up spoon*

    Present the child with a spoon. Score if he is able to pick up the spoon on or near the handle, banging it, dropping it, or moving it toward his mouth.

153. *Begins chewing movements with appropriate tongue motion*

   Observe the child eating foods with texture, such as cottage cheese, small cheese cubes, and cookies. Score if the child uses lateral tongue movements to push the food to either side of his mouth in a beginning chewing movement.

154. *Holds bottle to drink*

   Score if the child is able to hold and properly invert the bottle, making him independent at bottle-feeding time.

155. *Finger feeds small pieces of food*

   When given small bits of cereal, cracker, cheese, or meat, score if the child is able to feed himself with his fingers.

156. *Holds cookie*

   Score if, when given a cookie or cracker, the child is able to hold it and bring it to his mouth.

157. *Bites cookie*

   Score if the child is able to bite off a piece of cookie or cracker.

158. *Chews cookie*

   As the final step in this sequence, score if the child is able to chew and swallow the cookie pieces he has bitten off.

159. *Licks food off spoon*

   Dip a spoon in peanut butter, apple sauce, or other food that will cling to the spoon. Then hand the spoon to the child, letting him taste the food. Score if the child can lick the food from the spoon with his tongue.

160. *Eats mashed table foods*

   Score if the child no longer requires his food to be prepared in a special manner except by being mashed somewhat with a fork after being prepared as the rest of the family's meal.

161. *Ceases drooling*

   Score if the child no longer drools.

162. *Feeds self with spoon (many spills)*

   This indicates the start of independent spoon feeding. Score if the child is able to get food from his bowl to his mouth using a spoon, even though he may make a mess and his mother may finish feeding him the meal.

163. *Picks up and drinks from cup (some spilling)*

   Score if the child is able to pick up his cup, take a drink, and set the cup back down on the table, even though he may have difficulty controlling the flow of liquid from cup to mouth resulting in some spilling.

164. *Chews well*

   Score if the child is able to eat table food without any special preparation, such as mashing, and grinding, though foods may still have to be cut up in fairly small pieces.

165. *Drinks from cup without assistance*

   Score if the child requires no help in drinking from a cup and spills very little.

166. *Eats with spoon independently (entire meal)*

   Score if the child is able to feed himself his entire meal using a spoon without any assistance except for having food cut up somewhat, and completes the meal with little spilling.

167. *Discriminates edibles*

   Observe whether the child, in his play, mouths toys or places objects in his mouth. Score if the child uses his mouth only for edibles. (Thumbsucking, etc., should not be considered a failure on this item.)

168. *Unwraps candy; peels or pits fruit*

   This item is an extension of the last one, in that the child is now discriminating enough that he can be trusted not to swallow pits, bite through peelings, and can prepare simple fruits like bananas, or can spit out pits independently.

169. *Begins to use fork*

   Score if child can sometimes use a fork to pierce food particles and carry them to his mouth.

170. *Gets drink without help*

   Score if the mother indicates that at home the child is able to climb up to a faucet or reach a pitcher, pick up a glass, pour himself a drink, and get down again without any adult assistance, though there might be some spilling.

171. *Spoon feeds (no spilling)*

   This is the final extension of item number 162. This item is scored if the child handles a spoon without spilling or dropping food, and without overloading the spoon. The child may also be using a mature grasp of the spoon, but this is not necessary for scoring.

Toileting Skills

172. *Remains dry for 1 to 2 hour periods*

   Score if the child's diaper remains dry for 1 to 2 hour intervals.

173. *Fusses to be changed*

   Score if the child indicates both awareness that his diaper is wet or soiled and discomfort in that condition.

174. *Bowel movements are regular*

   Score if the mother indicates that the child has bowel movements at regular (not necessarily daily) intervals, occurring generally at the same time of day.

175. *Toilet training begins*

   Score if the child is ready for the child's mother to begin to toilet train him, that is, placing him on his toilet seat at regular intervals.

176. *Uses gestures or words to indicate need to toilet*

    This item is an extension of number 173 in that at this level the child is aware of sphincter pressure indicating the need to eliminate, rather than, as in number 173, simply has the knowledge that elimination has occurred. Score if the child indicates through words, gestures, moving toward the toilet that he is aware of his need to eliminate.

177. *Toilets independently except for wiping*

    Score if the child takes himself to the toilet without any cues other than his need to eliminate, undresses (except for difficult fastenings), uses the toilet, and dresses requiring no assistance except in cleaning himself.

178. *Seldom has bowel accidents*

    Score if the child generally uses the toilet independently for bowel movements.

Dressing/Hygiene Skills

179. *Pulls off hat, socks, or mittens on request*

    Score if the child pulls off his hat, socks, shoes, mittens, etc., when asked with verbal and possibly a physical prompt.

180. *Cooperates in diapering and dressing by moving limbs*

    Score if, during dressing, undressing, and diapering, the child extends and withdraws his arms and legs in such a way as to assist in the activity by making adaptive movements rather than struggling or resisting the activity.

181. *Attempts to brush hair*

    Give the child a comb or hairbrush. Score if he puts it to his hair in imitation of hair grooming.

182. *Imitates simple grooming actions with various objects, i.e., toothbrush, comb, washcloth, with little attempt to groom*

    This item is an extension of item number 181 reflecting the child's increasing knowledge of certain objects and their uses. Score if the child puts such articles to the proper body parts, imitating the activity rather than grooming himself.

183. *Undresses completely except for fastenings*

    Score if the child is able to completely undress himself, including shoes, socks, shirt and pants or dress, and underwear, upon request and without the need of any assistance except with fastenings and narrow neck openings.

184. *Attempts to put shoes on*

    Score if, upon request, the child attempts to put his feet in his shoes, whether or not he actually succeeds. The shoes may be interchanged, right to left, but the child should be placing his foot in the proper place in the shoe.

185. *Unzips and zips large zipper*

    Using the child's zippered jacket, a dressing board or dressing doll with a fairly large zipper, encourage the child to work the zipper. Score if he can move the zipper both up and down.

186. *Puts on simple clothes without assistance (hat, pants, shoes, etc.)*

Score if the child is able to perform at least two of these activities without any assistance: put shoes on his feet (not necessarily on the right feet), put on underpants, slacks, jacket, or socks. He need not be able to fasten the buttons, zippers, snaps, or other fasteners on the clothes.

187. *Washes and dries hands with assistance*

Score if the child is able to both wash and dry his own hands with an adult helping adjust the water, providing soap, and a towel.

188. *Dries hands independently*

Score if, after washing his hands, the child gets the towel and dries his own hands fairly free of water, returning the towel to its approximate place.

189. *Puts on coat, dress, T-shirt except for buttoning*

In this extension of number 186 the child is scored for being able to handle more difficult pieces of clothing, including T-shirts with snug neck openings, coats, and dresses. Thus, the child now should be able to put on most articles of clothing independently except for fasteners. Score if the mother reports that the child usually dresses himself independently.

190. *Undoes large buttons, snaps, shoelaces deliberately*

Score if the child is able to undress himself completely independently, including all accessible fastenings.

191. *Prone: turns head to either side*

    Score if, when the child is prone, he is seen to turn his head from side to side.

192. *Neck righting*

    With the child supine, turn his head to the side. Score if the child's body rolls as a whole in the direction of the head, with head and trunk maintaining alignment. Test to both sides.

193. *Upright: head bobs but stays erect*

    Hold the child upright on your lap, observing his head balance. Score if he can maintain his head in an upright position for a minimum of 15 seconds, even if it occasionally bobs toward his chest.

194. *Upright: negative support reaction (integration of stepping reflex)*

    Hold the child in an upright position. Touch the soles of his feet to a surface several times. Score if, after each time the surface is touched, the child holds his hips and knees in flexion and bears no weight on his feet.

195. *Prone: labyrinthine righting*

    With the child blindfolded, hold him suspended in the prone position. Score if the child raises his head vertically with his eyes and mouth horizontal.

196. *Prone: optical righting*

    Administer and score as in item number 195 but omit the blindfold.

197. *Prone: raises and maintains head at 45°*

    Place the child prone. Score if the child raises his head to and maintains it at 45° for a minimum of 20 seconds.

198. *Supine: kicks feet alternately*

    With the child supine and his legs free of constraints, observe his kicking movements. Score if the legs move in an alternating or reciprocal pattern.

199. *Integration of Moro reflex*

    Place the child halfway between the supine and sitting positions, supporting the child's head with your hand. Remove your hand allowing him to fall a few inches before catching his head. Score if there is no indication of the reflexive pattern of abduction and extension of the arms with opening of the hands.

200. *Prone: head and chest are raised to 90° with forearm support*

    Place the child prone and encourage him to lift his head. Score if the child is able to raise and maintain his head to 90° while supporting his weight on his forearms (puppy position) for a minimum of 60 seconds.

201. *Upright: bears small fraction of weight on feet*

    Hold the child upright. Score if he extends his hips and knees to accept some weight on his feet.

202. *Prone: props with extended arms*

Place the child prone. Score if the child clears his chest off the surface by supporting his weight on his hands with straightened elbows for a minimum of 30 seconds.

203. *Pulled to sitting with no head lag*

With child supine, offer him your hands or place your hands in his fists and give a brief, gentle tug. Score if child can control his head while being pulled to sitting and shows no initial head lag.

204. *Pulls self to sitting*

With child supine, offer him your hands or place your hands in his fists and give a brief, gentle tug. Score if the child pulls himself up, using your hands to stabilize himself.

205. *Prone: rolls to supine*

Place the child prone and encourage him to turn over. Score if he can roll from front to back deliberately. Do not score if the child rolls accidently.

206. *Prone: integration of tonic labyrinthine reflex (TLR)*

Place child prone. Palpate for increased tone in the flexors or watch for either the hips to automatically flex under the child or the head to resist being raised. Score if *none* of these conditions exist or the child spontaneously assumes the pivot prone position. *Note*: the presence of this reflex is uncertain in normal children but is present in cerebral-palsied children.

207. *Supine: integration of tonic labyrinthine reflex (TLR)*

Place the child supine and palpate for increased tone in the back and hip extensors or watch for the child's head to pull back, shoulders retract, hips and knees extend and hips adduct. Score if *none* of these conditions exist. Score also if the child is observed to bring hands to the midline or feet to the mouth. *Note*: the presence of this reflex is uncertain in normal children but is seen in children with motor problems.

208. *Prone: integration of symmetrical tonic neck reflex (STNR)*

With the examiner seated, place the child prone across your knees. Raise the child's head upright observing for changes in the positions of arms and legs. Observe whether the arms extend and the legs flex in response to head raising; or whether the arms flex and legs extend when the head is lowered. Score if no such indications exist.

209. *Supine: integration of asymmetrical tonic neck reflex (ATNR)*

Place the child supine and stimulate him to turn his head to one side, or turn his head passively. Note whether the arm on the side which the head is facing extends, with an increase of tone, while the opposite arm tends to flex in response to the head turning. Test to both sides. Score if no such indications exist.

210. *Sitting: trunk erect in chair*

Place the child in a high chair. Score if the child's head is kept upright and the trunk is straight while sitting.

211. *Upright: extends legs and takes large fraction of weight*

Administer as in number 201. Score if, when held in a standing position, the child straightens his legs and bears most of his body weight. This should not be confused with a pathological positive supporting reaction.

212. *Sits alone for at least 5 seconds*

Place the child in a sitting position. Score if the child sits independently for at least 5 seconds with the trunk essentially upright and with minimal hand support. There may be a slight lumbar curve.

213. *Supine: lifts head spontaneously*

Place child supine and extend your hands to him as if to lift him. Score if the child spontaneously lifts his head up off the surface while the rest of his body is still flat.

214. *Integration of neck righting*

Administer as in number 192. Score if the child does not roll immediately in the direction of the head turning.

215. *Body on body righting begins*

With the child supine, encourage him to roll over. Observe the rolling pattern. Score if he rolls segmentally, leading with shoulders, or hips, with the rest of the body following segmentally rather than in a totally aligned pattern as seen in number 192.

216. *Supine: labyrinthine righting*

With the child blindfolded, hold him in a suspended supine position. Score if the child lifts his head to the horizontal in alignment with his trunk.

217. *Supine: optical righting*

Administer as in number 216, omit the blindfold. Score to the same criteria.

218. *Prone: Landau reflex*

Hold the child in a suspended prone position. Score if the head, spine, and legs extend while in the position. *Note*: this reflex is difficult to evoke after age 1 and should be totally integrated by 2 to 2½ years.

219. *Sitting: protective extension to the front*

Place the child in a sitting position and lightly push him forward at the shoulders. Score if his arms come forward to protect himself from falling.

220. *Parachute reaction*

Hold the child at his waist and chest in a suspended prone position. Lower him head first toward the floor. Score if his hands come forward to touch the floor and protect his head from contact.

221. *Prone and supine: equilibrium reactions*

Place the child on a tiltboard in either a prone position or a supine position and tilt the board to one side. Score if his head and trunk move to the midline and the arm and leg on the raised side of the board abduct and extend while the opposite arm and leg show a protective extension reaction. Test to each side in both prone and supine positions.

222. *Sitting: labyrinthine righting when tipped to sides*

     With the child blindfolded, place him in a sitting position on your knees. Tip him to either side and score if his head is maintained at the midline with his eyes and mouth horizontal.

223. *Sitting: optical righting when tipped to sides*

     Administer as in number 222, omit blindfold. Score to same criteria.

224. *Supine: rolls to prone*

     Place child supine and encourage him to roll. Score if he rolls from back to front.

225. *Prone: pivots*

     Observe child while he plays in a prone position on the floor. Score if he is seen to extend both upper trunk and legs off the floor simultaneously, leaving only his stomach in contact with the floor. The child may turn somewhat in this position. He may use his arms or flex his knees in abduction to help him turn.

226. *Prone: crawls*

     Observe child in a prone position on the floor. Score if he propels himself forward for more than a few inches by moving both arms and legs while his stomach remains in contact with the floor.

227. *Sitting: protective extension to the sides*

     Administer as in number 219, this time pushing him gently to the side. Score if he extends an arm on that side to take his weight protecting himself from falling. Test on both sides.

228. *Standing: moves body up and down*

     Hold the child in a standing position on a solid surface and bounce him gently up and down on his feet. Score if he moves his body up and down by flexing and extending legs and hips.

229. *Sits unsupported for 60 seconds*

     Administer as in number 212, scoring if he meets the criteria while holding the position for at least 60 seconds.

230. *Prone or sitting: assumes quadruped position*

     Observe the child as he plays in a prone position on the floor. Score if the child raises himself on his hands and knees with his stomach well off the ground and maintains this position for a few seconds. Also score if the child assumes a hand-knee position from sitting.

231. *Quadruped: equilibrium reactions*

     While the child is in a quadruped position, gently push him to one side. Score if the head and trunk move to the midline and the arm and leg on the raised side abduct and extend while the opposite arm and leg show a protective extension reaction. Test on both sides.

232. *Sitting: assists in pulling upright*

     With child in a sitting or quadruped position, offer your hands and encourage him to pull himself to standing. Score if he pulls himself up to standing using the examiner's hands, with the examiner giving some support.

233. *Prone or quadruped: assumes sitting position*

Observe the child's activities while he plays in a prone or quadruped position on the floor. Score if he is able to assume the sitting position without external aids.

234. *Standing: raises one foot (attempts to step)*

Support the child in a standing position on a solid surface and encourage him to move forward. Score if he raises one foot in an attempt to step.

235. *Quadruped: creeps*

After administering number 230, encourage the child to move forward in the quadruped position. Score if he moves forward more than a few inches on hands and knees with stomach off the ground. Arms and legs should move in a reciprocal pattern.

236. *Sitting: protective extension to the rear*

Administer as in number 219, lightly pushing the child backward. Score if the child places his arms behind him to take his weight thus preventing his falling backward.

237. *Sits alone and steady for 10 minutes*

Score if the child sits well, with trunk erect and without need of hand support for at least 10 minutes. Give toys to the child to encourage him to stay in the position.

238. *Sitting: pulls to standing using furniture*

Set the child near a low table or chair and encourage him to pull himself up. Score if the child can pull himself to standing using the furniture without any other help.

239. *Standing: lowers self to floor*

After testing number 238, encourage the child to sit down again. Score if he intentionally lets himself fall in order to sit or lowers himself using the furniture.

240. *Standing: cruises by holding on to furniture*

With child standing at a low table, encourage him to move sideways. Score if he takes a few steps sideways while holding on to the table. Note to which side he moves.

241. *Walks with one hand held*

Score if the child can step comfortably with only one hand being held for balance.

242. *Sitting: equilibrium reactions*

Seat the child on a chair and pull him somewhat sharply to one side by his arm while stabilizing him at the hips. Score if the child's head and trunk move to the midline and the arm and leg on the raised side abduct and extend while the opposite arm and leg show a protective extension reaction. Test on both sides.

243. *Stands alone*

Place the child in a standing position and remove your support once he is balanced. Score if he is able to stand alone 3 to 5 seconds.

244. *Walks by himself*

   After testing number 241, encourage the child to come to you. Score if the child is able to take a few steps without support.

245. *Creeps up stairs*

   Place the child in a quadruped position at the foot of a shallow set of stairs and encourage him to climb them. Score if he is able to creep up two stair steps.

246. *Standing: throws ball with some cast*

   Demonstrate ball throwing and encourage him to imitate. Score if he releases the ball with some propulsion. Arms may move either in a horizontal or vertical direction and child need not control direction of ball.

247. *Walks well (stops, starts, turns)*

   Observe the child's walking. Score if he is seen to start and stop walking without need of a support and if he is able to change direction while he is moving.

248. *Supine: raises self to standing position independently*

   Place the child supine and encourage him to stand up. Score if he attains a standing position without need of support.

249. *Walks backward*

   Observe the child pulling a pull toy, and score if he walks backward as he watches the toy.

250. *"Runs" stiffly*

   Encourage the child to run. Score if he attempts running but with a stiff gait.

251. *Walks sideways*

   Score if the child is seen to walk sideways while pulling a pull toy or moving along a table.

252. *Walks up stairs held by one hand*

   Aid the child in walking up stairs by holding one hand. He may use a banister or wall to support his other hand. Score if he is able to ascend three or four steps with one hand held.

253. *Creeps backward down stairs*

   Place the child in a creeping position on the second or third step of a shallow staircase, encouraging him to descend the last two stairs. Score if he can creep down at least two stairs.

254. *Standing: seats self in small chair*

   While the child is walking about, encourage him to sit down in a child-sized chair. Score if he can seat himself, controlling the downward motion.

255. *Climbs into adult-size chair*

   Encourage the child to climb up into a standard-sized chair. Score if he manages to seat himself in the large chair.

256. *Standing: balances on one foot with help*

With the child standing in front of you, kneel down and encourage him to lift one foot as you hold his hand. Score if he can lift his foot for 2 or more seconds using your hand for support. Be sure to test both sides.

257. *Standing: equilibrium reactions*

With the child standing in front of you, move him forward, backward, and to each side with a quick movement at his shoulders. (He should be moved about 6 inches in each direction.) Score if the child's head and trunk move to the midline and the child takes short steps with the movement to maintain his balance.

258. *Walks down stairs with one hand held*

Administer as in number 252, encourage the child to descend three or four stairs holding your hand and the wall or banister for support. Score if the child is able to descend the stairs with one hand held.

259. *Squats in play; resumes standing position*

Observe the child as he moves about. Score if at any point he is observed to squat down and then resume a standing position without using anything for support or balance.

260. *Jumps in place*

Demonstrate jumping with both feet off the floor and encourage the child to imitate. Score if the child jumps off the floor with both feet clearing the floor simultaneously.

261. *Goes up and down stairs alone nonreciprocally*

Encourage the child to ascend and descend a few steps without any support. Score if the child is able to move up and down the steps by placing both feet on each step before proceeding to the next one. Child may use railing on a long flight of stairs. Note with which foot the child leads.

262. *Stands on balance beam with both feet; attempts to step*

Help the child stand on a 4-inch-wide balance beam. When he has his balance, encourage him to walk along the beam. Score if he balances well on the beam and attempts to step with minimal support from the examiner.

263. *Kicks ball*

Demonstrate kicking a medium-sized (8-inch diameter) ball. Place the ball in front of the child's foot and encourage him to kick the ball. Score if the child can lift one foot to kick the ball. Note with which foot the child leads.

264. *Jumps from bottom step (both feet together)*

Demonstrate jumping off a shallow step for the child. Encourage him to imitate. Score if he is able to jump with both feet in the air at the same time and land in a coordinated fashion (two-foot takeoff and landing).

265. *Walks on tiptoes*

Remove shoes and demonstrate walking on tiptoe for about 5 feet. Encourage the child to imitate. Score if the child is able to walk without his heels touching the ground for at least 10 feet.

266. *Throws ball 5 to 7 feet in a vertical pattern*

Demonstrate an overhand throw to the child and encourage him to imitate. Score if the child moves his arm in an overhand pattern releasing the ball high in the arc. The ball should move ahead 5 to 7 feet.

267. *Takes a few alternate steps on balance beam*

Administer as in number 262. Score if the child is able to take 2 or more alternate steps (forward foot changes) on the balance beam with minimal support.

268. *Supine: rises to standing with mature pattern*

Have the child lie on his back on the floor. Observe his method of rising to standing. Score if he sits straight up with minimal body twisting before he stands up.

269. *Rides tricycle using pedals*

Place child on a tricycle that allows him to place his feet comfortably on the pedals. Score if the child is able to pedal the tricycle forward 4 to 6 feet.

270. *Goes up stairs alternating feet*

Administer as in number 261. Score if the child ascends the stairs by placing only one foot on each step. Note with which foot the child leads.

271. *Stands on one foot and balances*

Demonstrate standing on one foot and encourage the child to imitate. See number 256 for other techniques. Score if the child is able to raise one foot and stand on the other, *without any support*, for 2 to 3 seconds. Be sure to test both sides.

272. *Walks with heel-toe gait*

Observe the child's walk. Score if child shows definite pattern of heel strike followed by push-off. Score both feet.

273. *Walks with reciprocal arm swing*

Have the child walk a distance of 8 to 10 feet. Score if pattern shows that the left arm and right leg move forward and backward together and that the right arm and left leg move together.

274. *Runs*

Observe the child running. Score only if both feet leave the ground for a fraction of a second during the pattern.

Program Development

From Assessment to Objectives

Behavioral objectives, i.e., specific statements about a positive change in one of a child's repertoire of skills which is expected to occur within a short period of time, formed the basis for both the individualized treatment programs and the group activities of the Early Intervention Project. Several aspects of behavioral objectives will be discussed, including the necessary components of an objective and the development of objectives based on assessment results from the *Early Intervention Developmental Profile*.

Components of an Objective

·Who Acts?
The first element of a behavioral objective is naming the actor, that is, the doer of the action. The following objectives all begin with a stated subject—the child—who is the actor.

1. **Ron** will lift his head to 90° and maintain it for 30 seconds when placed in a puppy position.

2. **Eleanor** will imitate the syllables ba-ba-ba-ba within 10 seconds of their presentation more than half the time.

3. **Walter** will point to four body parts on a baby doll when asked, *Where are the baby's____?*

A common error in objective writing is to name a subject who is not the actor. When this occurs, the objective has actually been written for someone else, and the subject is in fact the object, a passive participant. For example:

4a. **Ron** will have range of motion exercises daily for his hips, shoulders, wrists, and ankles.

Ron appears to be the subject of this objective, until we ask, *Who acts?* The actor in example 4a actually is whoever will be exercising Ron, and Ron is the passive participant in these exercises. If the above objective is rewritten to name the actor, it becomes the following:

4b. **Ron's mother** will perform range of motion exercises with Ron's hips, shoulders, wrists, and ankles.

Now we have a parent, or therapist, objective instead of a child objective. Thus, a child's objective should require that the child is the actor. After writing a child's objective, ask, *Who acts?* The answer should be the child.

·What Is the Action?
The second component of a behavioral objective is defining the action by using an active verb which clearly defines the behavior in question. A common error in objective writing is the use of nonspecific, rather than specific, verbs. For example, many words, such as tolerate, participate, recognize, improve, and understand, are nonspecific verbs which require the observer to make subjective decisions about the child's understanding, participation, recognition, or improvement based on the child's behavior. Instead of using indirect and unclear verbs, great care should be taken to specif-

ically describe the action which the subject will take. The following examples illustrate changing nonspecific to specific verbs:

5a. Chris **will tolerate** side-lying position for 5 minutes.

becomes

5b. Chris **will not cry** when positioned in side-lying for 5 minutes.

and

6a. Ken **will recognize** three pictures in his book *My Things*.

becomes

6b. Ken **will point to, name, touch** three pictures in his book *My Things*, when asked.

·What Is Being Acted On?

Now that we have an active subject and an active verb, we should examine the objective to see whether a direct object can be used. A few active verbs (intransitive verbs) do not take objects (see example 5b), but the vast majority of active verbs can be followed by an object. By specifically describing the direct object, ambiguity about the behavior in question can be reduced. Thus,

7a. Ken can point to **pictures** of objects when asked.

becomes

7b. Ken will point to **three pictures in his book *My Things***, when asked.

·To What Extent?

The fourth general component of writing objectives is establishing the criterion of the behavior, which is often expressed numerically in terms of how many (example 3), how often (example 8), how much of the time (example 2), or how long (examples 1 and 5b). For example:

8. Bill will urinate in his potty **three times a day** when placed on the potty every 2 hours. (How often?)

9. Linda will stack **six** 1-inch cubes. (How many?)

10. Carol will spoon-feed **half of each meal** without any help. (How much?)

·Under What Conditions?

A final, and extremely important, component needed when developing objectives for children with specific handicaps is indicating the physical conditions under which the behavior will occur. These conditions may include body positioning, adaptive equipment, or the child's physiological or emotional status, as noted in the following:

11. Lee will stand **in the parallel bars with extended hips** for 5 minutes **after relaxation**. (3 conditions)

12. Chris will lift her head and hold it at 90° for 3 minutes when **placed in prone position over a bolster**. (2 conditions)

Selecting Behaviors for Objectives

Now that the components of an objective have been described, let us consider the content of an objective, which reflects expected changes over a specific time period. Behavioral objectives for very

44

young children should focus on very small changes in behavior which are expected to occur within a given length of time (e.g., 3 months). The *Early Intervention Developmental Profile* provides a basis for selecting behaviors which are developmentally related. The process for determining which behaviors should be written as objectives begins with assessment of the child's present developmental skills in each area of functioning. Once the profile has been administered and the protocol completed, examination of the child's performance on each scale can begin. Attention should be given to the scores which fall between the basal and ceiling levels on each scale so that the age range in which consistent passes begin to become consistent failures can be determined.

Table 7 illustrates sample scores from the language section of the profile in which a child's passes change to failures in the 12 to 15-month-age range (transition area). Therefore, language objectives for this particular child should describe several language behaviors which are expected to emerge during the 12 to 15-month developmental period and which this child has not yet mastered.

TABLE 7

Scores Showing Transition Area from Which Objectives Are Selected

Age Range	Profile Item Number	Score
6-8 months	79	P
	80	P
9-11 months (basal level)	81	P
	82	P
	83	PF
12-15 MONTHS (TRANSITION AREA)	84	P
	85	F
	86	PF
	87	F
16-19 months (ceiling level)	88	P
	89	F
	90	F
	91	F

While the failed items on the profile protocol describe the behavior which will be incorporated into an objective, a real effort should be made to avoid rewriting the test item as an objective for the child. "Teaching the test" may move the child ahead on the assessment instrument, but it can create "surface" or "hollow" learning because the behavior has been taught as a splinter skill. Therefore, the underlying concepts of behaviors which form the basis for an item on the profile rather than the item itself, should be worked into behavioral objectives. For example, let us examine some possible behavioral objectives written for item 56 of the profile, *Shows knowledge of toy hidden behind a screen.* This task is described as the child's ability to search behind a propped book for a small toy. Writing the objective directly from the item description would result in something like this:

13a. Ken will reach behind a book which he has seen placed in front of a cracker and retrieve cracker consistently.

This objective contains the necessary elements, and after several months of practice Ken may be able to retrieve a cracker which has been placed behind a book. But, the item itself also taps the child's knowledge of simple spatial concepts which, in this case, are also dependent on the concept of object permanence for its success. In order to clearly pass this objective, the child needs to know (1) that the cracker continues to exist after he can no longer see it (object permanence), and (2) that the spatial relationships involved are the concepts of "behind" and "in front of." Ken may learn these concepts from practicing this one objective many times, but he may just as easily learn that knocking down the book will "magically" make a cracker appear. By focusing on an objective written directly from item 56, Ken may learn the required behavior without having formed the underlying spatial concepts required. If Ken's objective is rewritten using different behaviors to reveal the underlying spatial relationships, it would read:

13b. Ken will find a toy car when he sees his mother "drive" it behind her.

When Ken passes item 56 at the next assessment, his success on this item can be attributed to a generalization of the concepts of object permanence and spatial relationships which developed while working on objective 13b. His successful generalization implies acquisition of these necessary concepts rather than "splinter" learning of one particular task that has been repeated many times.

Thus, care should be taken to prevent profile items and item descriptions from being rewritten as behavioral objectives. Instead, a parallel behavior should be developed from the item, altering both the objects used and the specific activity. Success on the item in the future will then depend upon development of the general behavior pattern, rather than a specific behavior learned in isolation.

Developing Comprehensive Objectives

The child's *total* development should be the primary focus for programs which treat very young handicapped children. Too often programs focus on improving the major handicapping condition while ignoring other developing skills. For instance, a cerebral palsied toddler may be limited to physical therapy treatment for the first two years, and then receive speech therapy and occupational therapy attention once language and fine motor skills have developed. Such a program tends to ignore the cognitive and social realms and may seriously hamper a motorically involved child's intellectual progress. Programs for severely and profoundly retarded children have tended to focus intensively on self-care skills and somewhat on gross motor skills but have also tended to ignore the cognitive, social, and language areas because of these children's so-called low potential.

Program approaches which focus on the handicap or on a specific set of skills tend to foster several problems: (1) They encourage the child's development of "splinter skills" which may distort the true picture of the child's strengths and weaknesses. (2) They make teaching more difficult because the developmental prerequisites for the various skills are often not fully considered. For example, spoon feeding requires a combination of developmental skills in the areas of cognitive development (use of a tool [spoon] to transfer food from one place to another), fine motor development (shoulder, elbow, wrist, and finger coordination, as well as well-developed hand to mouth patterns), and oral motor development (proper mouth movements). Thus, attempting to teach spoon feeding before the child is developmentally ready in all these areas will prolong the teaching process by increasing the amount of help and the length of time he will need assistance, in addition to the frustration of teacher, parent, and child with the slow progress. And (3) single-approach programs tend to overlook abnormal patterns which may begin to emerge and which may interfere with the child's learning. Classrooms or residences for the severely retarded, blind, and motorically handicapped, for example, often provide little or no cognitive stimulation resulting in an environment in which the child is forced to supply his own stimulation as best he can. A child who resorts to self-stimulation with stereotypic behavior patterns will eventually have difficulty interacting with other objects in his environment.

Programs for very young handicapped children need to consider all facets of each child's development in order to create an atmosphere which will provide the cognitive, social, and language environment appropriate for that child while stimulating his motor development and his ability to manipulate objects. These latter skills form the basis for much of a child's learning during the sensorimotor period (Piaget, 1954). The child's level of social development provides guidelines for both the type and extent of adult interactions with him. The child who is socially younger than 6 months needs a different style of mothering than does the child whose social development is at the 12-month level. Staff members must be able to provide the kind of "mothering" which each child needs.

Likewise, knowledge of the child's cognitive development provides a guide as to which activities and objects will provide appropriate manipulation experiences for the child. And knowledge of the child's fine motor development allows the programmer to shape manipulation activities to fit the child's emerging capabilities.

Evaluation and programming based on the profile's six areas of development, perceptual/fine motor, cognition, language, social/emotional, self-care, and gross motor, assure a comprehensive and well-rounded program for handicapped infants. Two or three objectives for each area, focusing on different developmental tasks, will provide a comprehensive range of activities for the child, maintaining interest for him and his trainer(s), as well as providing many opportunities for success.

Even in a comprehensive program, there is often a tendency to stress the child's weakest area of development by writing most of the objectives in this area. Whenever there is a clear area of development which will continue to be frustratingly slow, the child's strongest area should be determined and stressed in the objectives. In this way the successes in the areas of strength can serve to balance the slow progress in other areas. A good rule of thumb is to write as many (or more) objectives in the stronger areas as are written in the weaker ones. Not only does this approach uplift the attitudes of those working with the child, but more importantly, it supports an area of development which the child may have to rely on to compensate for his handicap(s) in later life. A comprehensive program will focus on each child's potentially strongest areas while simultaneously treating the weaker areas.

Frequency of Writing Objectives

Because the behavioral objectives serve as the child's individual curriculum, evaluations should recur frequently (3 months is optimal) so that the effectiveness of his daily educational treatment program and his developmental "readiness" can be closely monitored. When objectives are written only once or twice yearly, the same activities, methods, and techniques are used for extended periods regardless of their effectiveness and are not adjusted to small changes in the child's functioning. Because the time it takes severely impaired children to develop new skills is so consuming, any time lost to inappropriate methods or goals is time that cannot be regained.

Evaluating and rewriting objectives every 3 months also reinforces parents and staff. In day to day contact it is difficult to see a child's progress. Little gains go unnoticed. Systematically evaluating a child every 3 months highlights the child's growth, and demonstrates the effectiveness of intervention to parents, therapists, and teachers.

The behavioral objectives for a 14-month-old cerebral palsied child are shown in table 8. Note the equal emphasis on her strongest areas, language and cognition, in addition to her weakest area, gross motor development. Note also that objectives have been written in each of the six profile areas to provide comprehensive programming and support for compensatory skills, even though this child is not delayed in cognitive, social, and language areas.

TABLE 8
Three-Month Objectives

Perceptual/Fine Motor

1. M. H. will replace all the "men in the bus" or pegs in a pegboard three out of five times they are presented.
2. M. H. will stack one toy on top of another successfully three out of five times.

Language

1. M. H. will point to what she would like when given a choice of two each time she is given a choice.
2. M. H. will point to four body parts (hair, eyes, toes, mouth) on herself upon request.
3. M. H. will label or point to three different pictures in a picture book when asked.

Cognition

1. M. H. will find a toy when hidden under one of two covers.

2. M. H. will try to imitate unfamiliar hand movements and sounds presented by her mother (need not be accurate imitations).

3. M. H. will successfully retrieve a toy from under the sofa using a wooden spoon.

Social/Emotional

1. M. H. will begin to interact actively with other children (i.e., rolling a ball to another child, reaching out or patting another child).

Self-care

1. M. H. will feed sticky foods (mashed potatoes or other vegetables) to self with a spoon.

2. M. H. will pull arms out of shirt with assistance and pull shirt over head independently.

3. M. H. will put brush to her hair in imitation of brushing her hair.

Gross Motor

1. M. H. will assume and maintain a kneel-stand position with minimal support from a person and will hold her balance for five seconds.

2. M. H. will completely roll from prone to supine and supine to prone when body on body righting is facilitated.

3. M. H. will reach up, forward, and laterally for a toy while sitting independently without falling over.

N. B. Early Intervention Project for Handicapped Infants and Young Children. These objectives relate to the July, 1975, assessment as noted on table 6.

From Objectives to Activities

Behavioral objectives developed from the profile not only serve as an individualized curriculum for a 3-month time period, but also become the basis from which a child's activities can be planned. The process of developing an objective from a profile item is described on pages 43-47. In order to choose a variety of activities which will stimulate the development of a skill, the behavioral objective must be examined in two ways. First, the underlying concepts or skills which the behavior expresses must be determined. Each underlying skill can in turn be used as an activity leading to the acquisition of the specific behavior named in the objective. Second, the purpose of the objects (toys) named in the objective must be determined. Alternate objects should be considered because using a variety of objects will not only maintain the child's interest but also promote generalization of activities from one object to another. Once the underlying skills and alternate objects are determined, they can be combined to form a set of activities which bears a strong relationship to the behavior named in the objective.

The following example illustrates these points:

Profile item 56:
    Shows knowledge of toy hidden behind a screen.

Behavioral objective:
    Ken will find a toy car when he sees his mother "drive" it behind her back.

Underlying concepts:
    1. object permanence (finds a hidden object; searches in place where a moving object disappeared)

    2. spatial relations (knowledge of "behind"; knowledge of "in front of")

    3. receptive language (understands "car" in *Where is the car?*)

    4. visual attention (can visually track moving object)

Alternate toys:
    book   small animal
    ball   crayon

cracker	spoon
key	rattle or noisemaker

Alternate screens:

pillow	bowl
blanket	dish
cookie sheet	high-chair tray
large toy	box

Alternate activities:

a. hiding a block first under a cup, then behind a cup

b. rolling a ball under a couch, or bed

c. slowly hiding a toy in various places (e.g., in a pants cuff, under a foot, in a sock)

d. holding an empty plate on its side as a screen and putting the child's cracker behind it

e. hiding a spoon in (under, behind, on top of, beside) a box

f. rolling a toy car a short distance under a blanket or pillow

Most objectives can be broken down into the underlying skills, as is shown above, and various objects and activities used to carry out the objective. Volume 3, *Stimulation Activities*, provides several activities for most items on the profile. Developed to be used by parents and paraprofessionals as well as by professionals, this detailed list of activities is designed to help parents learn the process by which objectives are translated into activities for their children.

Basic Activities and Program Ideas

Within each of the six developmental areas considered by the profile, there is a wealth of activities which occur naturally in the normal child's development and which can be successfully applied to programs for handicapped infants and young children. The Early Intervention Project's basic program approach for each of the six developmental areas included in the profile is discussed below with emphasis on methods used to teach a parent how to stimulate his child's development in each area.

Gross motor programming includes teaching parents how to move their child in and out of various positions, how to facilitate the development of normal reflexive postures, and how to hold their child correctly. Parents of a child with a severe motor handicap are taught various ways of positioning their child which would not only increase his head and trunk control, but also free his hands to explore objects, keep his spastic muscles relaxed, and give him the best view of activities going on around him. Special positions which facilitate feeding, bathing, and sleeping are also taught. In addition, parents are continuously encouraged to let their child explore and move about freely in a safe environment.

Perceptual/fine motor programming emphasizes the importance of multisensory stimulation. Parents are shown how to develop play activities by using a variety of media such as clay, sand, water, finger paint, textured fabric, and developmentally appropriate toys. Parents are encouraged to have a variety of objects available for the child to reach for, grasp, and manipulate. Rather than waiting for the child to spontaneously reach for objects, parents are taught how to motivate their child and how to demonstrate to the child what he is supposed to do. If the child does not learn through parent modeling, parents learn to prompt the child or move him through the activity so that the child always succeeds in accomplishing a task.

Cognitive programming is based upon a Piagetian framework of sensorimotor development in which emphasis is placed on sensory input to enhance perceptual and, later, conceptual development. Causality, spatiality, object permanence, and imitation are the four major tasks of each child's program. Activities, such as banging a spoon, shaking a rattle, pulling a string, or pushing a button which causes a toy to appear, help the child develop an understanding of the causes and their predictable effects. Dumping and filling activities, formboards, and pegboards are used to help a child learn the concept of spatiality which later emerges as body image, laterality and directionality. Playing peek-a-boo, watching where objects are dropped, and hiding and searching for toys are games which can help the child learn that objects exist even when they are no longer visible. This learning is critical to later emotional and conceptual development. In addition, children are taught to imitate vocal and motor actions. Because so much learning is accomplished through watching others and trying to mimic their behavior, teaching imitation is a major part of cognitive programming. Sounds, movements, and games which allow the child to watch and then imitate are used to develop this skill.

Self-care programs focus on the areas of dressing and undressing, feeding, and toileting. For many children, normal developmental sequences can be followed, and programs can be developed by analyzing the components of the behavior and teaching each in its appropriate sequence. However, many other children who are severely motorically involved require special procedures. For example, some parents are taught ways of positioning their child to eliminate unwanted reflexes since improper positioning may interfere with the child's achieving self-care independence and may turn self-help activities into unpleasant chores which give no pleasure to either parent or child. Proper feeding procedures are particularly important. For many cerebral palsied infants, feeding becomes a long, exhausting process which is unrewarding to both parent and child. If, however, the child is relaxed and properly positioned, mealtime can provide a time for a comfortable, warm interaction between parent and child.

The development of attachment between child and parent is the most important *social/emotional* task in the early years of life. Helping parents work comfortably with their children plays a key role in allowing them to be nurturing, spontaneous, and loving. Parents can learn to notice and respond to their child's needs, and to eventually become less self-conscious about their interactions with their child while allowing both the child and themselves to grow in the relationship.

Language is the final area of programming. Parents are taught how to facilitate both expressive and receptive language development in their child's growing repertoire. Parents are encouraged to talk to their child about things around them, about their actions, and about the child's actions. They are taught to use key words consistently and to pair them with actions, feelings, and events. Parents are also taught to listen to their child, to imitate the sounds he makes, and to expand his repertoire of words and phrases. Parents learn how to use books with their young child by pointing to pictures and helping the child attach labels to things he sees. By becoming part of the child's daily play, puppets, records, games, rhymes, and songs can help develop both speech and language.

·Home Activities

One essential element of the Early Intervention Project's educational philosophy is that parents are the best teachers for their own handicapped infants and young children. Although parents are given considerable assistance by a professional team, they remain the primary deliverers of service to their child. In order to assure 24-hour treatment for their child and to make it feasible for parents to play strong therapeutic roles, parents are assisted in making the child's treatment part of their daily routine. Parents learn to incorporate suggested activities into the family's routine so that they can capitalize on the therapeutic potential of all their interactions with the child. Since the entire family system is viewed as the client, siblings, grandparents, babysitters, and others close to the family are also taught how to handle the handicapped child therapeutically.

In order to effectively incorporate the child's objectives into a routine, it is first necessary to have an idea of the daily household schedule, particularly as it involves the child. Not only should the programmer know when the child wakes, eats, naps, plays, and goes to bed, but also when his parents or caretakers can devote a specific amount of time to the child. Many objectives can be used with most daily activities.

8:00   Breakfast (eating objectives)

9:00   Bath time (hygiene objectives; range of motion and other therapeutic exercises; and dressing objectives)

9:30   Playtime (cognitive; perceptual/fine motor; and/or gross motor objectives)

10:30   Nap

12:00   Lunch (eating objectives)

1:00   Playtime (language, cognitive, and/or perceptual/fine motor objectives)

3:00   Nap

4:30   Playtime with siblings, father, and others (gross motor objectives)

6:00   Supper (eating objectives)

7:00   Bedtime story (language objectives)

In addition to the play periods which can incorporate objectives into the natural play of the child with his family, other activities, such as gross motor (i.e., ways to position, carry, and lift the child) and social can be carried out during each contact with the child and can gradually become second nature to the family. Since parents vary in their abilities to incorporate therapeutic/educational objectives into their home routine, they may need assistance in adapting the home environments and schedules to better meet the needs of their handicapped child. Regular home visits by an interdisciplinary team member can be extremely helpful in aiding a family to carry out their child's objectives at home. The home visitor can take note of the available objects, toys, and furniture that will be needed for the child before recommending purchase of special toys or adaptive equipment. For instance, towels and blankets make excellent bolsters; a coffee table can serve as a support for a child learning to cruise; kitchen cupboards are storehouses of interesting objects for a child who can sit.

Therapeutic activities, such as range of motion exercises or postural drainage, can be handled much the same as those relating to the objectives. One major difference stands out: while most objectives can be incorporated into the child's everyday play with family members and can be carried out, altered, or discarded as determined by the child's interest and skills, some therapeutic activities must be carried out whether or not the child is cooperative. It is critical that parents understand the importance of therapeutic activities and that they be monitored frequently to make sure the procedures are carried out correctly. The home visitor can teach parents various ways of incorporating therapeutic activities into rhymes, songs, and movements that make them more enjoyable for the child. Carrying out therapeutic activities at the same time of day, such as before or after bathtime, may decrease the child's resistance by making these activities routine and expected.

·Group Activities

A combined home- and center-based program benefits a professional staff because it provides at least two environments in which a handicapped child can be observed and activities planned. It benefits the child by giving him exposure to more children and adults; and it benefits the parents by giving them opportunities to share experiences with other parents "who have been there," and to observe a broad range of handicapped children, some of whom are more handicapped than their own child, some of whom are less handicapped. A group session can give parents the chance to compare their child with his peers rather than to a normal population; to highlight their child's strengths and special gifts; and to see their child in a different, more positive way.

When bringing children and parents together for a group session, two elements are important: (1) children and their parents should work in small groups in which a similar activity is appropriate for each child, rather than having a parent/child work in isolation as is the situation at home; and (2) staff members should circulate freely, observing the children, working with them and their parents intermittently, and altering and adapting activities to meet the therapeutic/educational needs of each child.

During a group session a nonambulatory child may work with his own parent(s) and near one or two other parent-child sets. Toddlers, however, may be encouraged to interact with other children while their parents provide them with interesting materials to explore independently. The group program for toddlers who are developmentally at the 24 to 36-month level can be planned around the profile's six areas of development, with their individual objectives in each area incorporated into the group activity. Thus, a 2-hour session for a toddler-level group might be scheduled as follows:

9:00–9:20	Free play (social objectives)
9:20–9:40	Perceptual/fine motor activities
9:40–10:00	Language activities
10:00–10:20	Snack time (self-care objectives)
10:20–10:40	Cognitive activities
10:40–11:00	Gross motor activities

Altering Activities for Specific Handicaps

Intervention programs for handicapped infants and toddlers can expect to have a population of severely damaged children, since milder handicaps are often not diagnosed until the later preschool years. More than half the treatment group in the Early Intervention Project had multiple handicaps which generally consisted of mental retardation (brain damage) in combination with motor and/or sensory handicaps. The most severely neurologically damaged children demonstrated all three handicaps: severe retardation, severe motor handicaps, and sensory impairment.

Traditionally, treatment/education programs for handicapped children have grouped children according to their handicap and in the process have excluded most children with retardation accompanied by a sensory or motor handicap. There are strong arguments for separate educational programs for school-aged children (over age 5) with severe motor or sensory handicaps. These programs are based on the child's educational potential and on different educational techniques that are needed, particularly for the sensory-impaired children. The tasks which severely handicapped children with normal intelligence must master are varied and require different approaches (i.e., oral training of the hearing-impaired; Braille for visually impaired; physical adaptations needed by motorically impaired).

However, the same arguments to not apply to the very young handicapped child. The developmental tasks for the handicapped infant and toddler are more similar than different when considering all handicaps. The development of fine and gross motor skills, social/emotional growth, and cognitive gains appear to follow the same patterns regardless of the handicapping condition, though the rate and style may be altered. A program which focuses on comprehensive developmental stimulation can accommodate children with all types of handicapping conditions, meeting their individual needs with individualized program objectives. Group sessions and parent training strengthen the long-term effects of such a program. By mixing handicaps, the deaf child can be surrounded by hearing children (the nonmobile child by mobile children, etc.), and stimulation can be provided for each child in the area where it is most needed.

Subgrouping may be necessary when the children span different developmental levels. Subgroups which were used by the Early Intervention Project were:
1. *Young infants:* children who can not sit alone and who have no locomotion patterns. Programming for this group tends to focus on head and trunk control, grasp and reach patterns, visual and auditory localization, and vocalizations.
2. *Older infants:* children who can sit, roll, grasp, and begin to manipulate objects. Programs focus on the beginnings of purposeful activity, grasp and release, motor and vocal imitation, object permanence, cause-and-effect relations, and early balance and prewalking activities.
3. *Toddler group:* children who are walking. This group needs separate space for their increased activity, mobility, and need for independence. This group needs to be separated from groups 1 and 2 which can be easily combined. Toddler programs tend to focus heavily on language activities, perceptual/fine motor tasks (puzzles, shape discriminations, and

crayon activities), eating, toileting, and dressing skills. Motor activities stress higher equilibrium and coordination responses.

Motorically Impaired Child

Proper handling and positioning of a motorically involved child is of prime importance and must be constantly considered. It is recommended that a physical or occupational therapist have frequent and regular input into a handicapped infant program so that the individual requirements of each child can be carefully monitored. The child's position should be determined by each activity. The cerebral palsied infant can be put in a prone position over a bolster to facilitate head and trunk control, but this position may not be appropriate for some fine motor activities. The child may respond better in a side-lying position which may reduce increased arm tone and thus free his arms for fine motor activities. It is possible to reduce increased muscle tone with proper positioning and relaxation techniques and thus enable the child to have maximum control over his gross motor, fine motor, and oral motor movements. On the other hand, stimulation of muscle tone and positioning techniques can increase tone in the hypotonic (floppy) child.

When asking the motorically involved child to perform fine motor or oral motor activities, every attempt should be made to normalize muscle tone which may interfere with the child's response to the activity. The child should be positioned to inhibit pathological reflexes with the head and trunk supported so that the child can pay attention to his hand or mouth movements. Various facilitation positions are thoroughly discussed by Finnie (1975).

Once the child is well positioned, the materials must be presented to the child in such a way that minimal movement produces maximal results. The child should be assisted in movements only to the extent necessary for action to occur. Activities which require minimal movement for effects include: knocking down stacked blocks; making noise with a toy piano, bell, rattle; water play; toys fastened to the child's wrists; and toys which make sounds when tapped. In addition to gross and fine motor responses, the programmer should be aware of more subtle responses with which the severely motorically involved child can indicate learning and communication. For example, when the head is free and trunk is well supported, *head movements* may demonstrate the child's ability to localize sound, look in response to his name, and identify various noisemakers. *Eye pointing* responses may indicate many receptive language skills (e.g., child looks at the named object, picture, or person) as well as object permanence concepts. Since receptive and expressive language skills may develop at different rates due to oral motor involvement, emphasis should be placed on differentiating *receptive language* skills using eye pointing and head responses from *expressive language* skills where vocal, and then verbal, imitation are extremely important. (It should be noted that oral motor performance, whether eating or vocalizing, can be severely affected by spasticity. Proper positioning, relaxation, and desensitization techniques should be a part of all language and feeding activities.) Communication boards can also be used for receptive and expressive language activities when the oral motor mechanisms are severely affected.

Adaptive equipment plays an important part in the motorically impaired child's treatment program. Because it is important that the physically handicapped child be a part of his peer group during activities, special devices may be necessary to seat the child in an upright position so he can see and hear the activities around him. Very often the motorically impaired child can be found on a floor mat or slumped in a high chair thereby isolating him from the rest of the children who are involved in activities elsewhere in the classroom.

Visually Impaired Child

As with the motorically involved child, proper handling of a blind child is a primary concern because of his dislike of movement. The lack of movement thus results in gross motor developmental delay, particularly in ambulation. Treatment should focus on developing the child's adaptability to various environments by using familiar objects, people, or routines to help the child distinguish and identify several different environments. The child's feeling of comfort should be of utmost importance as he is placed in prone or sitting positions, or moved through space. But movement should be part of his daily routine from very early in life since blind children tend to spend much time on their backs if not properly stimulated.

Since tactile and auditory senses must become the blind child's major sources of sensory information, care should be taken to provide organized, yet contrasting, tactile and auditory experiences for the child. Since sound will probably be the blind child's motivation for movement, auditory localization, reaching toward sounds, and auditory discrimination skills should be a major part of the blind child's program. Even though language is an important informational source and should not be overlooked especially as babbling and imitation skills emerge, language is a secondary informational source for the blind child and should not be considered as a replacement or substitute for tactile, manipulatory, and auditory experiences.

Particular care should be taken to make sure the blind child always has interesting toys at his fingertips and that they are changed frequently. Boredom quickly leads to stereotypic behavior patterns which the child may later use instead of more goal-directed behaviors which provide the stimulation he needs. He should not be left without adult intervention for more than short periods, whether alone or in a group. The adult must be sensitive to the lack of organized stimuli in a group situation and be able to interpret the environment for the blind child; he must also be ready to provide new stimuli when the child is alone since he is already isolated by the nature of his handicap. The blind child, more so than other children, requires an attending adult who must provide a screening and organizing function, and who can modulate sensory input so the child is neither overwhelmed nor bored. With proper adult support, the blind child should achieve self-directed activity and independence.

Hearing Impaired Child

The very young hearing impaired child is the least limited of the three handicaps considered here since his visual and motor sensory modes are predominant in the early period of sensorimotor learning. When language becomes a major basis for learning and interacting, the hearing impaired child begins to have problems. Therefore, early preparation of the deaf infant and toddler focuses on preparing him to communicate. Eye contact is primary since it is by sight that the child will compensate for being unable to hear. Also, as with the blind child, organization of the sounds surrounding the child is quite important. In order for the hearing impaired child to utilize any residual hearing, he must experience clear differences in sound patterns rather than constant background noise which effectively blankets any hearing discriminations he might learn. Tapes, records, and noisy toys can all provide important hearing experiences for the child, provided they are presented in an organized manner.

Professional consultation with audiology and speech and language therapy is crucial for the hearing impaired infant and toddler so that the communication mode which will be used with him can be decided upon and incorporated into all his experiences. Teaching families about communication systems and techniques to use them are lengthy processes and must begin early in order to give the child a communication mode by the time he is cognitively ready to use it. Professional consultation will be needed to recommend and monitor hearing equipment which is often used with infants and toddlers.

Activities for the hearing impaired child are similar in the early years to normal developmental sequences since the child's visual, tactile, and motor skills are intact. These skills need particular attention, however, since they will form the basis for the child's later compensations. The deaf preschooler probably benefits the most from categorical grouping once he is ready to learn a communication system, since it is such specialized learning. Preschools for hearing impaired children should be considered by the time the child is 2 especially since more and more deaf education programs now begin with 2 or 3 year olds. Again, professional consultation with the speech and language therapist working with the child is useful in making this decision.

Appendix

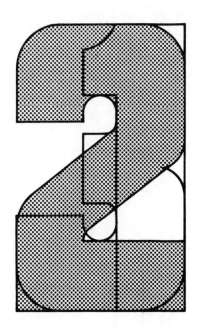

Developmental Programming for Infants and Young Children

D. Sue Schafer and Martha S. Moersch, Editors

Early Intervention Developmental Profile

by Sally J. Rogers, Diane B. D'Eugenio, Sara L. Brown,
Carol M. Donovan, and Eleanor W. Lynch

		1	2	3	4	
Chronological Age						Name _____
						Birthdate _____
						Referring Problem(s) _____
						Tested by
Evaluation Dates						1. _____
						2. _____
						3. _____
						4. _____

Perceptual/Fine Motor

Name _____

Item Number	DEVELOPMENTAL LEVELS AND ITEMS	Date	Date	Date	Date
	0-2 Months				
1	Follows moving object past midline				
	3-5 Months				
2	Integration of grasp reflex				
3	Reaches for dangling object				
4	Moves head to track moving object				
5	Fingers own hands in play at midline				
6	Uses ulnar palmar prehension				
7	Looks at hands				
8	Reaches for cube and touches it				
9	Uses radial palmar prehension (uses thumb and two fingers)				
10	Transfers toy from hand to hand				
	6-8 Months				
11	Retains two cubes after third is offered				
12	Rakes or scoops up raisin and attains it				
13	Has complete thumb opposition on cube				
14	Pulls one peg out of pegboard				
15	Uses inferior pincer grasp with raisin				
	9-11 Months				
16	Pokes with isolated index finger				
17	Drops blocks imitatively with no pause before release				
18	Uses neat pincer grasp with raisin				
19	Attempts to scribble (holds crayon to paper)				
20	Holds crayon adaptively (crayon projects out of radial aspect of the hand, one end up and one end down)				

Developmental Programming for Infants and Young Children
Volume 2: Early Intervention Developmental Profile

Perceptual/Fine Motor

Item Number	DEVELOPMENTAL LEVELS AND ITEMS	Date	Date	Date	Date
	12-15 Months				
21	Turns page of cardboard book				
22	Removes cover from small square box				
23	Places one or two pegs in pegboard				
24	Builds two-cube tower				
25	Scribbles spontaneously (no demonstration)				
	16-19 Months				
26	Places six pegs in pegboard without help				
27	Builds three-cube tower				
28	Places round form in formboard (three forms presented)				
29	Imitates crayon stroke (crayon gripped with butt end firmly in palm)				
	20-23 Months				
30	Places six pegs in pegboard in 34 seconds				
31	Makes vertical and circular scribble after demonstrations				
32	Completes three-piece formboard				
33	Builds six-cube tower				
34	Begins to manipulate crayon with fingers				
35	Folds paper imitatively				
	24-27 Months				
36	Draws vertical and horizontal strokes imitatively				
37	Aligns two or more cubes for train, no smokestack				
	28-31 Months				
38	Builds eight-cube tower				
	32-35 Months				
39	Copies a circle already drawn				
40	Cuts with scissors				

Developmental Programming for Infants and Young Children
Volume 2: Early Intervention Developmental Profile

Cognition

Name _____

Item Number	DEVELOPMENTAL LEVELS AND ITEMS	Date	Date	Date	Date
	0-2 Months				
41	Uses adaptive movements rather than reflexive reactions				
	3-5 Months				
42	Demonstrates vocal contagion				
43	Repeats random movements (primary circular reactions)				
44	Watches place where moving object disappeared				
45	Coordinates two actions in play				
	6-8 Months				
46	Attains partially hidden object				
47	Looks to the floor when something falls				
48	Uncovers face				
49	Rotates a bottle inverted less than 180° to drink				
50	Acts to have pleasurable interaction repeated				
51	Imitates sounds or hand movements already in his repertoire				
	9-12 Months				
52	Pulls string to secure ring and succeeds				
53	Imitates facial movements inexactly				
54	Attains completely hidden object (single visible displacements)				
55	Imperfectly imitates sounds and movements never performed before				
56	Shows knowledge of toy hidden behind a screen				
57	Rotates a bottle inverted 180° to drink				
	13-18 Months				
58	Repeatedly finds toy when hidden under one of several covers (multiple visible displacements)				
59	Balances eight 1-inch cubes in a coffee cup				

Developmental Programming for Infants and Young Children
Volume 2: Early Intervention Developmental Profile

Cognition

Item Number	DEVELOPMENTAL LEVELS AND ITEMS	Date	Date	Date	Date
60	Lifts a 1/2-inch cube off a 1-inch cube cleanly, with pincer grasp				
61	Inverts a small vial in order to retrieve raisin				
62	Uses a stick to try to attain an object out of reach				
63	Uses trial-and-error approach to precisely imitate new sounds, words, or movements				

19-23 Months

64	Deduces location of object from indirect visual cues (invisible displacements)				
65	Anticipates trajectory by detouring around object				
66	Imitates sounds, words, or body movements immediately and exactly without practicing				
67	Indicates knowledge of cause-effect relationships				

24-29 Months

68	Matches colored blocks (red, yellow, blue, green, black)				
69	Pretends to be engaged in familiar activities (being asleep, telephoning)				
70	Understands concept of one				

30-36 Months

71	Repeats two digits				
72	Matches four shapes (circle, square, star, cross)				
73	Identifies objects by their use (car, penny, bottle)				

Developmental Programming for Infants and Young Childr
Volume 2: Early Intervention Developmental Pro

Name _____   # Language

Item Number	DEVELOPMENTAL LEVELS AND ITEMS	Date	Date	Date	Date
	0-2 Months				
74	Moves limbs, head, eyes in response to voice, noise				
	3-5 Months				
75	Vocalizes when talked to or sung to				
76	Turns head in direction of voices and sounds				
77	Vocalizes emotions, intonation patterns				
78	Exhibits differentiated crying				
	6-8 Months				
79	Imitates speech sounds				
80	Forms bisyllabic repetitions (ma-ma, ba-ba)				
	9-11 Months				
81	Waves or claps when only verbal cue is given				
82	Imitates nonspeech sounds (click, cough)				
83	Inhibits activity in response to *no*				
	12-15 Months				
84	Uses appropriate intonation patterns in jargon speech				
85	Imitates words inexactly				
86	Uses two words meaningfully				
87	Uses gestures and other movements to communicate				
	16-19 Months				
88	Shows body parts, clothing items, or toys on verbal request				
89	Labels one object				
90	Follows two simple directions				
91	Uses single words to express wants				
92	Points to several body parts (on self or doll)				

Developmental Programming for Infants and Young Children
Volume 2: Early Intervention Developmental Profile

Language

Item Number	DEVELOPMENTAL LEVELS AND ITEMS	Date	Date	Date	Date
93	Names one black and white picture				
94	Selects two of three common objects				

20-23 Months

95	Begins using simple two-word sentences				

24-27 Months

96	Uses first name when referring to self				
97	Uses three-word sentences				
98	Uses negation, *no*				
99	Uses simple pronouns (I, me, you, mine)				
100	Labels at least three common objects or pictures				

28-31 Months

101	Demonstrates an understanding of two prepositions				
102	Understands body part functions				

32-35 Months

103	Says first and last names				
104	Demonstrates an understanding of three prepositions				
105	Forms questions spontaneously using a verb				
106	Follows two-step commands				
107	Forms or uses plurals				

Developmental Programming for Infants and Young Children
Volume 2: Early Intervention Developmental Profile

Social/Emotional

Item Number	DEVELOPMENTAL LEVELS AND ITEMS	Date	Date	Date	Date
	0-2 Months				
108	Quiets when picked up				
109	Quicts to face and voice				
110	Maintains brief periods of eye contact during feeding				
111	Smiles or vocalizes to talk and touch				
	3-5 Months				
112	Reflects adult's smile without verbalizing				
113	Laughs				
114	Cries when left alone or put down				
115	Shows awareness of strange environments				
116	Reaches to familiar people (discriminates strangers)				
117	Likes physical play				
118	Smiles spontaneously				
119	Smiles at image in mirror				
120	Watches adult walk across room				
	6-8 Months				
121	Laughs at pat-a-cake and peek-a-boo games				
122	Withdraws or cries when stranger approaches				
123	Shows dislike when familiar toy is removed				
124	Pats and touches mirror image				
	9-11 Months				
125	Shows discomfort when separated from mother in strange environment				
126	Participates in pat-a-cake and peek-a-boo games				
127	Repeats vocalizations or activity when laughed at				
128	Offers toy but does not release				

Developmental Programming for Infants and Young Children
Volume 2: Early Intervention Developmental Profile

Social/Emotional

Item Number	DEVELOPMENTAL LEVELS AND ITEMS	Date	Date	Date	Date
	12-15 Months				
129	Offers and releases toy to adult				
130	Initiates ball play or social games				
	16-19 Months				
131	Uses mother as secure base, checking back with her frequently				
	20-23 Months				
132	Occasionally plays near other children				
133	Often clings to or pushes away adult				
134	Cries when preferred activity is blocked				
135	Picks up and puts away toys on request				
	24-27 Months				
136	Independently chooses toy and begins to play				
137	Prefers to play near, but not with, other children				
138	Mimics domestic activities				
	28-31 Months				
139	Stares at or points to sexual differences				
	32-35 Months				
140	Separates from mother easily in strange environment				
141	Identifies own sex				
142	Begins to understand taking turns				

Developmental Programming for Infants and Young Child
Volume 2: Early Intervention Developmental Pro

Name _____

Self-care

Item Number	DEVELOPMENTAL LEVELS AND ITEMS	Date	Date	Date	Date
Feeding Skills	**3-5 Months**				
143	Sucks and swallows pureed foods from spoon				
144	Integration of rooting reflex				
145	Coordinates sucking, swallowing, and breathing				
146	Anticipates feeding with increased activity				
147	Gums or mouths pureed food				
148	Integration of bite reflex				
	6-8 Months				
149	Gums and swallows textured food				
150	Closes lips on spoon to remove food				
151	Drinks from cup with help				
152	Begins to pick up spoon				
153	Begins chewing movements with appropriate tongue motion				
154	Holds bottle to drink				
	9-11 Months				
155	Finger feeds small pieces of food				
156	Holds cookie				
157	Bites cookie				
158	Chews cookie				
159	Licks food off spoon				
160	Eats mashed table foods				
161	Ceases drooling				
	12-15 Months				
162	Feeds self with spoon (many spills)				
163	Picks up and drinks from cup (some spilling)				
164	Chews well				
	16-19 Months				
165	Drinks from cup without assistance				
166	Eats with spoon independently (entire meal)				
167	Discriminates edibles				
	20-23 Months				
168	Unwraps candy; peels or pits fruit				

Developmental Programming for Infants and Young Children
Volume 2: Early Intervention Developmental Profile

Self-care

Item Number	DEVELOPMENTAL LEVELS AND ITEMS	Date	Date	Date	Date
	24-35 Months				
169	Begins to use fork				
170	Gets drink without help				
171	Spoon feeds (no spilling)				
	Toileting Skills **12-15 Months**				
172	Remains dry for 1 to 2 hour periods				
173	Fusses to be changed				
	16-23 Months				
174	Bowel movements are regular				
175	Toilet training begins				
	24-35 Months				
176	Uses gestures or words to indicate need to toilet				
177	Toilets independently except for wiping				
178	Seldom has bowel accidents				
	Dressing/Hygiene Skills **12-15 Months**				
179	Pulls off hat, socks, or mittens on request				
180	Cooperates in diapering and dressing by moving limbs				
181	Attempts to brush hair				
	16-19 Months				
182	Imitates simple grooming actions with various objects, i.e., toothbrush, comb, washcloth, with little attempt to groom				
	20-23 Months				
183	Undresses completely except for fastenings				
184	Attempts to put shoes on				
185	Unzips and zips large zipper				
	24-31 Months				
186	Puts on simple clothes without assistance (hat, pants, shoes, etc.)				
187	Washes and dries hands with assistance				
	32-35 Months				
188	Dries hands independently				
189	Puts on coat, dress, T-shirt except for buttoning				
190	Undoes large buttons, snaps, shoelaces deliberately				

Name _____

Gross Motor

Item Number	DEVELOPMENTAL LEVELS AND ITEMS	Date	Date	Date	Date
0-2 Months					
191	Prone: turns head to either side				
192	Neck righting				
193	Upright: head bobs but stays erect				
194	Upright: negative support reaction (integration of stepping reflex)				
195	Prone: labyrinthine righting				
196	Prone: optical righting				
197	Prone: raises and maintains head at 45°				
198	Supine: kicks feet alternately				
3-5 Months					
199	Integration of Moro reflex				
200	Prone: head and chest are raised to 90° with forearm support				
201	Upright: bears small fraction of weight on feet				
202	Prone: props with extended arms				
203	Pulled to sitting with no head lag				
204	Pulls self to sitting				
205	Prone: rolls to supine				
206	Prone: integration of TLR				
207	Supine: integration of TLR				
208	Prone: integration of STNR				
209	Supine: integration of ATNR				
6-8 Months					
210	Sitting: trunk erect in chair				
211	Upright: extends legs and takes large fraction of weight				
212	Sits alone for at least 5 seconds				
213	Supine: lifts head spontaneously				
214	Integration of neck righting				

Developmental Programming for Infants and Young Children
Volume 2: Early Intervention Developmental Profile

Gross Motor

Item Number	DEVELOPMENTAL LEVELS AND ITEMS	Date	Date	Date	Date
215	Body on body righting begins				
216	Supine: labyrinthine righting				
217	Supine: optical righting				
218	Prone: Landau reflex				
219	Sitting: protective extension to the front				
220	Parachute reaction				
221	Prone and supine: equilibrium reactions				
222	Sitting: labyrinthine righting when tipped to sides				
223	Sitting: optical righting when tipped to sides				
224	Supine: rolls to prone				
225	Prone: pivots				
226	Prone: crawls				
227	Sitting: protective extension to the sides				
228	Standing: moves body up and down				
229	Sits unsupported for 60 seconds				
230	Prone or sitting: assumes quadruped position				
231	Quadruped: equilibrium reactions				
232	Sitting: assists in pulling upright				
233	Prone or quadruped: assumes sitting position				
234	Standing: raises one foot (attempts to step)				

9-11 Months

Item Number	DEVELOPMENTAL LEVELS AND ITEMS	Date	Date	Date	Date
235	Quadruped: creeps				
236	Sitting: protective extension to the rear				
237	Sits alone and steady 10 minutes				
238	Sitting: pulls to standing using furniture				
239	Standing: lowers self to floor				
240	Standing: cruises by holding onto furniture				
241	Walks with one hand held				
242	Sitting: equilibrium reactions				
243	Stands alone				

Developmental Programming for Infants and Young Children
Volume 2: Early Intervention Developmental Profile

Item Number	DEVELOPMENTAL LEVELS AND ITEMS	Date	Date	Date	Date
	12-15 Months				
244	Walks by himself				
245	Creeps up stairs				
246	Standing: throws ball with some cast				
247	Walks well (stops, starts, turns)				
248	Supine: raises self to standing position independently				
249	Walks backward				
	16-19 Months				
250	"Runs" stiffly				
251	Walks sideways				
252	Walks up stairs held by one hand				
253	Creeps backward down stairs				
254	Standing: seats self in small chair				
255	Climbs into adult-size chair				
256	Standing: balances on one foot with help				
257	Standing: equilibrium reactions				
	20-23 Months				
258	Walks down stairs with one hand held				
259	Squats in play; resumes standing position				
260	Jumps in place				
	24-27 Months				
261	Goes up and down stairs alone nonreciprocally				
262	Stands on balance beam with both feet; attempts to step				
263	Kicks ball				
264	Jumps from bottom step (both feet together)				
	28-31 Months				
265	Walks on tiptoes				
266	Throws ball 5 to 7 feet in a vertical pattern				

Developmental Programming for Infants and Young Children
Volume 2: Early Intervention Developmental Profile

Gross Motor

Item Number	DEVELOPMENTAL LEVELS AND ITEMS	Date	Date	Date	Date
267	Takes a few alternate steps on balance beam				
268	Supine: rises to standing with mature pattern				

32-35 Months

Item Number	DEVELOPMENTAL LEVELS AND ITEMS	Date	Date	Date	Date
269	Rides tricycle using pedals				
270	Goes up stairs alternating feet				
271	Stands on one foot and balances				
272	Walks with heel-toe gait				
273	Walks with reciprocal arm swing				
274	Runs				

Developmental Programming for Infants and Young Children
Volume 2: Early Intervention Developmental Profile

Profile Graph

Name _____   Birth Date _____

Evaluation Dates _____

Developmental Level in Months	Perceptual/ Fine Motor	Cognition	Language	Social/ Emotional	Self-care			Gross Motor
					Feeding	Toileting	Dressing	
32-35	40* 39	73	107 ↑ 103	142 ↑ 140	171		190 ↑ 188	274 ↑ 269
28-31	38	72 71	102 101	139	170	178	187	268 ↑ 265
24-27	37 36	70 ↑ 68	100 ↑ 96	138 ↑ 136	169	177 176	186	264 ↑ 261
20-23	35 ↑ 30	67 ↑ 64	95	135 ↑ 132	168	175	185 ↑ 183	260 ↑ 258
16-19	29 ↑ 26	63 ↑ 	94 ↑ 88	131	167 ↑ 165	174	182	257 ↑ 250
12-15	25 ↑ 21	↑ 58	87 ↑ 84	130 129	164 ↑ 162	173 172	181 ↑ 179	249 ↑ 244
9-11	20 ↑ 16	57 ↑ 52	83 ↑ 81	128 ↑ 125	161 ↑ 155			243 ↑ 235
6-8	15 ↑ 11	51 ↑ 46	80 79	124 ↑ 121	154 ↑ 149			234 ↑ 210
3-5	10 ↑ 2	45 ↑ 42	78 ↑ 75	120 ↑ 112	148 ↑ 143			209 ↑ 199
0-2	1	41	74	111 ↑ 108				198 ↑ 191

Profile item numbers

*Developmental Programming for Infants and Young Children
Volume 2: Early Intervention Developmental Profile*

The following short-term goals, activities, and adaptations are excerpted from volume 3, *Stimulation Activities.*

Developmental Age	**3-5 Months**	Perceptual/Fine Motor

Short-term goal

Child will reach for dangling object or noisemaker.   *Eye-hand Coordination*

Activities

Put a toy or rattle in a place where the child's arms will make contact with it when he moves his arms.

Hang a brightly colored ball above the child's crib low enough so that he can touch it when he reaches up.

Shake a rattle or bell beside the child. Encourage him to reach for it.

Dangle the child's favorite toy or put a mobile above his crib. Encourage him to reach for it.

Before picking the child up, put your arms out to him to encourage the child to reach for you. Help him reach up and forward if he does not do it on his own.

> **Hearing Impaired**: *Attract the child with bright colors and textures rather than noisemakers.*
>
> **Motorically Involved**: *Present the object at midline and guide the child's arm toward the toy.*
>
> **Visually Impaired**: *Use items, such as a mobile or ball, which make a noise when only slightly moved.*

Developmental Age	**9-12 Months**	Cognition

Short-term goal

Child will pull a string or stick to attain an object.   *Causality*

Activities

Tie an object (rattle, light pull toy, ring) to one end of a string and the child's wrist to the other. Demonstrate pulling on the string to get the object. Encourage imitation.

Demonstrate the use of a push-pull toy (toy attached to a stick). Help the child pull until he gets the idea. Decrease assistance as the child gains skill.

Tie an object to a string and show the child how to *get it.* Be sure the object is out of reach and that the string is near the child. Encourage imitation.

Use any pull toy to strengthen this skill, such as quacking ducks, or a ringing fire engine.

Note: Tie a large wooden bead to the end of the string opposite the toy. This may make it easier for the child to hold on to the string and pull it.

> **Hearing Impaired**: *Use an object that is very visually stimulating (e.g., toy engine that puffs smoke as it is pulled).*
>
> **Motorically Involved**: *Only minor adaptations are necessary to make the activities appropriate.*
>
> **Visually Impaired**: *Make sure the object at the end of the string makes a noise when it is moved.*

Developmental Age	12-15 Months	Language

Short-term goal

Child will point to an object named or wanted.   *Reception*

Activities

Ask the child, *Where's your hat?* or *Where's the dog?* and observe how he answers you. If he attempts to go to the object, say, *Yes, there it is* and point to the object.

When the child pulls at you or fusses for attention, ask him what he wants. If he does not point, you point to several locations you think appropriate (refrigerator, toy, water faucet) and encourage him to do so.

Put three or four toys or items of food in front of the child; ask him, *Where is the* (baby)? and encourage him to point.

> **Hearing Impaired**: *When the child points or gestures, encourage him to get the object he needs by pushing him gently in the appropriate direction and holding objects up for him to accept or reject.*

> **Motorically Involved**: *If the child is unable to reach or point, encourage him to eye point to the object named.*

> **Visually Impaired**: *Encourage the child to name the item wanted. Ask him if he wants familiar things such as milk, juice, cookie, bell.*

Developmental Age	20-23 Months	Social/Emotional

Short-term goal

Child will play near other children on occasion.   *Social Play*

Activities

Invite friends' children to your home. Put your child near the children to watch them play. Encourage him when he responds by moving toward them or sitting by them.

Take your child to the park and encourage him to watch and imitate the other children.

Share babysitting with a friend who has children. Encourage your child to watch and play near these children.

Note: Children at this age do not generally play *with* others or share toys. They can, however, learn to imitate other children's play and may move closer as they become more comfortable with the situation.

> **Hearing Impaired**: *Introduce your child to the other children, explaining to them that he does not hear well.*

> **Motorically Involved**: *If the child cannot crawl or move well, place him in a position where he can watch children walking home from school, playing, and in TV programs.*

> **Visually Impaired**: *Encourage the other children to play with noise toys and to talk to your child. Explain to them that he does not see well.*

Developmental Age   **24-31 Months**   Self-care

Short-term goal

Child will indicate need to toilet.   *Toileting*

Activities

Note when elimination occurs and determine whether it is signaled by any specific behavior (facial expressions, genital handling). When pretoileting behavior is shown, immediately place the child on the toilet and reward any elimination.

When you are taking the child to the toilet, use a consistent word, such as *potty*, to indicate the activity and encourage the child to imitate.

Whenever you see the child displaying any signaling behavior, respond with the consistent word for the toilet so that the child will learn the connection and quickly place him on the toilet.

Do not scold the child for soiling. Reward him when he remains dry.

> **Hearing Impaired:** *Use a label or sign consistent with the alternative communication system.*

> **Motorically Involved:** *Seek aid from professionals regarding adaptive toileting equipment.*

> **Visually Impaired:** *Spend much time introducing the child to the potty chair. Let him sit on it for very brief periods at first to avoid excessive fear.*

Developmental Age   **16-19 Months**   Gross Motor

Short-term goal

Child will "run" or walk very fast.   *Walking*

Activities

Introduce games of fetching objects so the child "runs" to retrieve a ball and bring it back to you.

Play catch me or chase games to encourage the child to move quickly.

Demonstrate running and encourage child to imitate you.

CAUTION: Discontinue this activity if the child tends to walk on his toes during normal activities until you have consulted with a doctor or therapist.

Note: This goal is the first step toward moving quickly while maintaining balance and precedes true running which occurs at a later age.

> **Hearing Impaired:** *Only minor adaptations are necessary to make the activities appropriate.*

> **Motorically Involved:** *Only minor adaptations are necessary to make the activities appropriate.*

> **Visually Impaired:** *These children need to gain confidence in moving about familiar surroundings. Introduce running in a barrier-free environment when child seems ready, so the child will be assured of not running into unexpected obstacles.*

Selected Bibliography

Anderson, R.; Miles, M.; and Matheny, P. *Communicative Evaluation Chart from Infancy to Five Years*. Cambridge: Educator's Publishing Service, 1963.

Banham, K. *Quick Screening Scale of Mental Development*. Brookport: Psychometric Affiliates, 1963.

Barnard, Kathryn E., and Powell, Marcene L. *Teaching the Mentally Retarded Child*. St. Louis: C. V. Mosby, 1972.

Bayley, Nancy. *The Bayley Scales of Infant Development*. New York: Psychological Corporation, 1969.

Bobath, Karel. *The Motor Deficit in Patients with Cerebral Palsy*. Lavenham: Lavenham Press Limited, 1969.

Bower, T. G. R. "The Object in the World of the Infant." *Scientific American* 225 (October, 1971): 30-38.

Bowlby, John. *Attachment*. (Attachment and Loss Series, vol. 1). New York: Basic Books, 1969.

———. *Separation: Anxiety and Anger*. (Attachment and Loss Series, vol. 2). New York: Basic Books, 1973.

Bzoch, Kenneth R., and League, Richard. *The Receptive-Expressive Emergent Language Scale for the Measurement of Language Skill in Infancy*. Gainesville: Tree of Life Press, 1971.

Caplan, Frank, ed. *The First Twelve Months of Life: Your Baby's Growth Month by Month*. New York: Grosset and Dunlap, 1973.

Cattell, Psyche. *Infant Intelligence Scale*. New York: Psychological Corporation, 1940.

Cratty, Bryant. *Perceptual and Motor Development in Infants and Children*. New York: Macmillan, 1970.

Doll, Edgar A. *Measurement of Social Competence: A Manual for the Vineland Social Maturity Scale*. Minneapolis: American Guidance Service, 1953.

———. *Preschool Attainment Record: A Preschool Scale of Development*. Minneapolis: American Guidance Service, 1966.

Farber, Shereen D., and Huss, A. Joy. *Sensorimotor Evaluation and Treatment Procedures for Allied Health Personnel*. Indianapolis: Indiana University Foundation, 1974.

Finnie, Nancie R. *Handling the Young Cerebral Palsied Child at Home*. 2d ed. New York: E. P. Dutton and Company, 1975.

Fiorentino, Mary R. *Reflex Testing Methods for Evaluating C. N. S. Development*. Springfield: Charles C. Thomas, 1972.

Fraiberg, Selma. *The Magic Years*. New York: Charles Scribner's Sons, 1959.

Frankenburg, William K., and Dodds, Josiah B. *Denver Developmental Screening Test*. Denver: University of Colorado Medical Center, 1969.

Gesell, Arnold; Halverson, Henry M.; Thompson, Helen; Ilg, Frances L.; Castner, Burton M.; Ames, Louise Bates; and Amatruda, Catherine S. *The First Five Years of Life*. New York: Harper and Row, 1940.

Giblin, Paul. "The Development of Imitation in Piaget's Sensory-motor Period of Infant Development (Stages III-VI)." Master's thesis, Ohio State University, 1971.

Gratch, G., and Landers, W. F. "Stage IV of Piaget's Theory of Infant's Object Concepts: A Longitudinal Study." *Child Development* 42 (1971): 359-72.

Griffin, Patricia M. *Learning Accomplishment Profile for Infants*. Chapel Hill: University of North Carolina's Chapel Hill Training-Outreach Project, 1975.

Hedrick, D. L., and Prather, E. M. *Sequenced Inventory of Language Development*. Seattle: University of Washington's Child Development and Mental Retardation Center, 1970.

Hoskins, T. A., and Squires, J. E. "Developmental Assessment: A Test for Gross Motor and Reflex Development." *Physical Therapy* 53 (1973): 117-25.

Illingworth, R. S. *The Development of the Infant and Young Child: Normal and Abnormal*. Baltimore: The Williams and Wilkins Company, 1973.

Knobloch, Hilda, and Pasamanick, Benjamin. *Developmental Evaluation in Infancy*. Columbus: Division of Child Development, Ohio State University, 1966.

———, ed. *Gesell and Amatruda's Developmental Diagnosis*. 3d ed. Hagerstown: Harper and Row, 1974.

Leiter, R. *The Leiter International Performance Scale*. Chicago: Stoelting, 1969.

Mahler, Margaret; Pine, Fred; and Bergman, Anni. *Psychological Birth of the Human Infant*. New York: Basic Books, 1975.

Mecham, Merlin J. *Verbal Language Development Scale*. Minneapolis: American Guidance Service, 1971.

Mecham, Merlin J.; Jex, J. L.; and Jones, J. D. *Utah Test of Language Development*. Salt Lake City: Woodruff Printing and Litho, 1967.

Mysak, Edward D. *The Neuroevolutional Approach to Cerebral Palsy and Speech*. New York: Teacher's College Press, 1968.

National Association for Retarded Children. *Helpful Guide in the Training of a Mentally Retarded Child*. Virginia: Department of Health, Bureau of Child Health, 1968.

Pearson, Paul H., and Williams, Carol E. *Physical Therapy Services in the Developmental Disabilities*. Springfield: Charles C. Thomas, 1972.

Piaget, Jean. *The Construction of Reality in the Child*. New York: Basic Books, 1954.

——. *Plays, Dreams, and Imitation in Childhood*. New York: W. W. Norton, 1962.

Rogers, Sally J. "Factors Affecting Sensorimotor Development in Profoundly Retarded Children." Ph.D. dissertation, Ohio State University, 1975.

Sanford, Anne R. *Learning Accomplishment Profile*. Chapel Hill: University of North Carolina's Chapel Hill Training-Outreach Project, 1973.

Shirley, Mary M. *The First Two Years: A Study of Twenty-Five Babies*. Vol. 1. *Postural and Locomotor Development*. Minneapolis: University of Minnesota Press, 1931.

Spock, Benjamin. *Baby and Child Care*. New York: Pocket Books, 1968.

Stutsman, R. *Merrill-Palmer Scale of Mental Tests*. New York: Harcourt, Brace and World, 1948.

Terman, L. M., and Merrill, M. A. *Stanford-Binet Intelligence Scale*. New York: Psychological Corporation, 1967.

Thomas, A.; Chesni, Y.; and Dargassies, S. *The Neurological Examination of the Infant*. London: National Spastics Society, 1960.

Wechsler, David. *Wechsler Preschool and Primary Scale of Intelligence*. New York: Psychological Corporation, 1967.

Zimmerman, I.; Steiner, V.; and Evatt, R. *Preschool Language Scale*. Columbus: Charles E. Merrill, 1969.